Survival Skills
for the
Modern
Man

LIFE · LOVE · WORK · PLAY

Donn M. Davis

CB

CONTEMPORARY BOOKS

Library of Congress Cataloging-in-Publication Data

Davis, Donn M.
    Survival skills for the modern man : life, love, work, play / Donn M.
Davis.
       p.   cm.
   ISBN 0-8092-2973-0
    1. Single men—Life skills guides.   2. Bachelors—Life skills
guides.   I. Title.
HQ800.3.D38   1998
646.7′0086′52—dc21

                                            98-5655
                                            CIP

Cover and interior design by Scott Rattray
Cover and half-title page image copyright © Stephanie Rausser/FPG International LL
Interior Illustrations by Precision Graphics

Published by Contemporary Books
A division of NTC/Contemporary Publishing Group, Inc.
4255 West Touhy Avenue, Lincolnwood (Chicago), Illinois 60646-1975 U.S.A.
Copyright © 1998 by Donn M. Davis
Printed in the United States of America
International Standard Book Number: 0-8092-2973-0

18   17   16   15   14   13   12   11   10   9   8   7   6   5   4   3   2

To Sharon, who rescued me from
the throes of bachelorhood

Contents

Introduction

CARY GRANT AND Dean Martin had it. Joe Namath, Ted Turner, Jack Nicholson, and Michael Jordan have it. Each a man's man. Each a ladies' man. They made their mark with style.

Life for the regular guy is not as simple as it was for our forefathers. These days there are too many rules, too many demands, too much competition for the things we want. The goal of this book is simple: to give you the tools you need to get ahead, to impress others, to live the good life. In this book are all the basics a man needs to know in today's world in forty-seven easy doses. Promise.

The modern man doesn't need to know everything. He does, however, need to *appear* to know everything. He must know enough tricks of the trade to be confident as he sets out to get what he wants. He must be able to both land the girl and lose the girl, if necessary. He needs to know how to climb the corporate ladder and stay up there. He needs to be resourceful, able to do everything from painting a room to making an omelette to reading the stock tables. He should be schooled in the finer things in life—cigars, music, parties, toys. He should be a sharp gambler, an avid sportsman. He must look the part, with the right clothes, the right physique. He must act the part—sometimes a swinger, sometimes a tycoon, sometimes a gentleman. And he must do it all with style.

Survival Skills for the Modern Man was written to give you the cheat sheet, the answer key to get what you want. Filled with tips, guidelines, and rules about life, love, work, and play, it's an unconventional look at the don't-dos, the should-dos, and the must-dos that most guys face today. I think you'll find it an informative and opinionated guide, and I know it will help any guy master the art of being a man.

Survival Skills
for the
Modern
Man

Part I

Women and Dating

Forty-Four Basic Rules

"There are two ways to handle a woman,
and nobody knows either of them."
—*Kin Hubbard*

SOME THINGS ARE not open to debate. They just are. Follow these forty-four rules on how to treat a woman . . . no matter what. Break them at your own peril.

1. Don't leave the toilet seat up at night.

2. If you say you'll call, call.

3. Don't talk about ex-girlfriends, even when she "really wants to know."

4. Your car, big-screen TV, and killer stereo are much more interesting to you than they are to her.

5. Boxers, not briefs.

6. Watching sports on TV is not a date.

7. Learn to like "chick flicks."

8. Kids are cute and would be great to have when your future wife is ready.

9. Don't lie to her.

10. If you do lie to her, make sure it is for a damn good reason.

11. Don't tell her you lied to her—that's what deathbeds are for.

12. Don't cheat.

13. Machismo can be a good thing.

14. Be a good listener (or at least be able to look as if you're listening).

15. Her siblings must like you.

16. Her friends must think you are a catch.

17. Her parents must think you are the right religion.

18. Remember *all* anniversaries (including first sighting, first date, and engagement).

19. Pick her up at the airport.

20. She cares if you are in shape.

21. Not shaving on weekends is sexy.

22. Not shaving generally is not.

23. Kissing is important.

24. Nobody was ever a better lover than she is.

25. Always walk her to the door.

26. She doesn't want another beer as much as you do.

27. Cook for her—she'll appreciate the effort.

28. Humor probably does not come naturally to her, so give her the benefit of the doubt.

29. Don't look over her shoulder at a passing girl.

30. The answer to the question "Do I look heavier?" is always "no."

31. The answer to the question "Do you like what I'm wearing?" is always "yes."

32. You're a cat person, too.

33. A little Frank Sinatra or John Coltrane on the CD goes a long way.

34. Admit when you're wrong.

35. Take her work seriously.

36. Male bonding is good.

37. Male bonding on a Saturday night is bad.

38. She wants presents, lots of presents, no matter what she says.

39. A sweater is not an acceptable gift.

40. Taking her shopping for her own gift is worse.

41. Tiffany's is good.

42. Don't tell her that you love her if you don't.

43. If you do love her, tell her often.

44. Keep smilin'.

These rules may not be fair, but they are rules—live by them and prosper.

Getting That First Date

"A man chases a woman until
she catches him."

—*Proverb*

IF YOU CAN'T meet 'em, you can't get 'em out on a date, you can't build a relationship, you can't bring 'em home . . . you get the point. You've got to get first dates. Without first dates, your social life will continue to consist of steak dinners with the guys and ESPN. Not bad supplements, but not the stuff to build your social life around.

How many times have you said to your buddies, "Why is that babe with that loser?" Lots of times. The reason that babe is with that loser is that he drove to the hoop, unafraid of rejection. No real mystery, no need to change who you are—it's just confidence and effort. So, grab your little black book and memorize these time-tested tricks to meeting women.

1. **Fish where the fish are.** It's hard to meet women if you spend your weekend nights watching action videos or playing poker. You've got to be where the women are. Take a bike ride along the lake. Go to black-tie charity mixers. Accept qualified fix-ups. Hit the bars, but watch the girls, not the tap. Don't ever discount the opportunities around you. Health clubs, grocery stores, and weddings all offer casual opportunities to strike up a nonthreatening rap. True, you must act fast and be creative in these situations, but why miss any chance?

2. **Play your own game.** Women can sniff out a fake. If you're a macho, ball cap–wearing guy, be one. If you're a fast-talking jokester, use it. A fraternity

brother of mine used his "shy guy" routine to great success. He stood back against the wall while others danced the night away. He was polite and unassuming at first meeting. After a while, he would ask a girl if she wanted to take a walk outside to get away from the commotion. He even admitted—as the closer— that he was a shy guy. It was his game, and it was natural, charming, and successful.

3. **Use available props.** She drops her sunglasses on the floor—pick them up and say hello. She is folding her laundry—plop yours down on the same folding table and strike up a conversation. Loan her a quarter for the jukebox and pick out songs together. Ask to borrow the extra bar stool from her table, and stay for a few minutes. Most one-on-one situations such as these offer easy icebreakers. They are casual, friendly. They help you be you and help you take that first step toward meeting her.

4. **Engage her interest.** Just as you have a few canned answers ready to go for a successful interview, have a few easy conversation pieces in your repertoire. Perhaps an interesting story that plays up your importance at work. Maybe a funny story about your childhood. Lighthearted current events are always good. If you can't think of a funny, charming, and brief story about yourself, tell a funny, charming, and brief story about someone else.

5. **Act like a friend.** I know, you don't need another friend, especially a woman. Well, neither does she. It's just a pretense. Oftentimes, it makes a woman more comfortable while she decides if she likes you and you meet her criteria. This is especially important when chasing coworkers and women already in serious relationships. These women want to go out but need a socially acceptable cloak. Give it to her—let her know

you are not interested in dating anyone right now but would like to see her if it is OK with her that *you are just going out as friends.* (Be careful here, though—if you are *too* nice you won't get the girl.)

6. **It's shots on goal.** The Red Wings won the Stanley Cup converting an average three of thirty shots on goal. Tony Gywnn has won seven batting titles getting on base one out of every three times. Guys who don't introduce themselves generally don't meet girls. Guys who don't ask girls out generally don't get dates. Remember, the worst that can happen is a no. Think of it as the cost of doing business. Over time you will get more confident, raising your conversion percentage, your average. While your friends laugh next Friday at your four flameouts, you'll smile, knowing your fifth try got you that one great phone number.

Love on the Internet

"You've got mail, baby, yeah!"

—*Mike Myers as* Austin
Powers, International
Man of Mystery, *in an*
AOL *celebrity greeting*

THE INTERNET HAS changed everything. On-line services allow you to do just about anything you need in life without leaving your favorite couch. You can plan and book your travel to Bali. You can manage your banking, bills, and investments. You can buy music, flowers, even groceries. But can you consummate the ultimate transaction on the Internet—finding a woman? You bet your sweet 56 KB modem you can.

Finding a mate on-line offers many advantages. First, an on-line personal ad is often free. Second, the Internet allows for longer listings than most printed classifieds, a real bonus for those who feel that they can't adequately describe how wonderful they are in thirty words or less. Third, it allows lonely hearts to meet with more anonymity. On the World Wide Web, people can meet and chat behind clever E-mail addresses, never exchanging real names or phone numbers.

"Sportsaholic, potentially alcoholic, workaholic seeks sex-pot to do errands, have kids, and adore him."

Before you go looking for love in all the Web places, think about who you are and how to present yourself. Describe the traits that make you stand out. Everyone is handsome, athletic, and funny (or certainly everyone *says* he is). Too many people like weekends in the country and honesty. Outline the unique traits that will appeal to the kind of women you really hope to attract.

"Boring fat guy with few prospects seeks beautiful blonde with trust fund."

Realize that your personal ad is your first and oftentimes last chance to make the sale. You'd better set a persuasive hook, or you will lose the fish. Don't just say you like staying in: say you like staying in with two bottles of fine merlot, lots of chilled Godiva chocolates, and taped *X-Files* episodes. Be proud you're into Thursday-night disco at Club Underground. If you like a woman soft as Malo Cashmere, let it be known.

"Man with little going for him seeks anyone."

One of the best ways to meet and greet the fairer sex via the Internet is in chat rooms, such as those offered on America Online (AOL). Chat rooms are accessible twenty-four hours a day, seven days a week. Each chat room has its own topic and personality, and conversation ranges from easygoing to downright sleazy. Look around and find a room that suits your purpose. On-line interaction has its own language and etiquette, so it's a good idea to simply observe the chat room dialogue for a while before you jump in.

Along with chat rooms, there are more than 500 sites on the Internet designed for people who are looking to hook up with that special someone. Use Yahoo (www.yahoo.com) or Excite (www.excite.com) to locate the current hot sites. Almost all Internet personals sites offer the capability to narrow the field for your perfect match. Type in "stunning, curvy, rich, sophisticated, sports loving, funny, easygoing, and presentable to parents"—and you are likely to get a few listings. Add "available" and you will certainly get none. The Internet can help you find a woman, but it can't create miracles.

Selecting Music for the Seductive Evening

"When words leave off, music begins."
—*Heinrich Heine*

SONNY AND CHER—no; Frank Sinatra—yes. The right music sets the mood for seduction. The wrong music destroys it. The trick is matching the woman to the song. One type of music, or even one particular artist, can be one woman's aphrodisiac and another's aloha.

Think of the music you select as a reflection of you. Who does she want to be with? Harry Connick, Axl Rose, Randy Travis, or Miles Davis? If you are not sure what the moment calls for, give one of these a spin.

Jazz

Pretty much a can't-miss music choice. Sexy, hip, smoky. Even if she doesn't like jazz, she will like you for playing it.

1. John Coltrane—*Giant Steps*

2. Miles Davis—*Kind of Blue*

3. Stan Getz—*Best of the West Coast Sessions*

4. Chet Baker—*With Fifty Italian Strings*

5. Duke Ellington—*The Blanton-Webster Band*

Crooners

Second only to jazz in timeless, universal effectiveness. Crooners speak for those who are hopefully too tongue-tied to speak for themselves.

1. Harry Connick Jr.—His stuff all sounds about the same; pick one.

2. Nat King Cole—*Greatest Hits*

3. Frank Sinatra—*Sinatra 80th: All the Best*

4. Sam Cooke—*Man & His Music*

5. Tony Bennett—MTV *Unplugged*

Classical/New Age/Postmodern

A tough one. Depending on your date's taste, this selection can either make or break the night. Well, punk, do you feel lucky?

1. Ravel—*Bolero*

2. David Byrne—*Oh Samba*

3. George Winston—*Autumn*

4. Rachmaninoff—*Concerto No. 3*

5. Philip Glass—*Powaaqatsi*

Rock

Sometimes there is no substitute for a head-banger's ball. Rock is generally best played loud on a sweaty summer evening. It is also good in the car. Here are five of my favorites from the '60s, '70s, and '80s.

1. Elvis—*Top Ten Hits Volume 1 and 2*

2. Prince—*Purple Rain*

3. Van Morrison—*Best of Van Morrison*

4. Rod Stewart—*Unplugged*

5. Queen—*Greatest Hits*

The volume of the music is as important as the selection itself. Two of my best seduction memories are dominated by sound volume. In one case, my Yamaha was pumping a robust 100 watts through the Bose 900s so loud I would not have heard the police break down my door. In the other, the music was so soft I could hear the congo rhythm of my nervous heart.

Keep this in mind, too: not all situations are better with music. The sound of silence worked for Dustin Hoffman, and sometimes it can work for you.

The Art of the Kiss

"You kiss by the book."

—*Romeo and Juliet*

SHE FLIPS HER hair back, she laughs a little more, her hand lingers on your arm, she bends down and reveals just a little cleavage, her voice takes on a creamy quality, her eyes are bright. She likes you. She is ready for you to kiss her. *It is time for a kiss.*

Kissing is the only sexual act in which man and woman communicate in exactly the same way. Each brings a set of lips, a mouth, and a tongue. Both give and take. Kissing is the most intimate act, one that can unite the hearts as well as ignite the libidos. All the more reason to take your craft seriously.

Kissing, of course, may not properly be taught by a book. Nonetheless, informal polling of women yields the following basic dos and don'ts of the kiss. Obviously, there is a lot more room for experimentation as the relationship develops and you and your lover develop a wonderfully unique smooch style.

DO look into her eyes *before* the kiss. The look may be intense, romantic, friendly, or seductive, as your personality and the situation merits.

DON'T look into her eyes (or anywhere else, for that matter) *during* the kiss until the relationship is comfortable.

DO kiss like a man, not a New Age wimp—whatever that means.

DON'T miss the chance to make it vocal. Saying something just before or right after you kiss will demonstrate your playfulness and confidence.

DO make it last as long as you can, and as long as you sense she's willing. There is no need to cut the kiss short due to shyness or an arbitrary time limit.

DON'T just pay the kiss lip service once you're sleeping together—the kiss is a basic in any great sexual encounter. Never treat it as an annoying pit stop on the way to the orgasm finish line. Kiss her as if kissing her is the goal unto itself.

The Etiquette of Public Kissing (and Other Displays of Affection)

Some of your most memorable times can be had in public— a long cab ride, under a beach blanket, in a bathroom during a party. Whether and how much to engage in public demonstrations of *amore*, however, depend upon your accurate assessment of two factors: the character of the woman, and the nature of the public situation.

Regarding the first factor, a woman generally reacts to public displays of affection in one of three ways: (1) with comfort and even enthusiasm, (2) with discomfort and even rejection, or (3) with hesitation but appreciation and a willingness to be coaxed. A few respectful forays should give you a good idea of your steady's normal response.

As for the second factor, ask yourself the following questions: Just how visible are the two of you? Are you among friends, family, associates, or strangers? How relaxed or formal is the occasion? How distracting would your actions be to others? How bad do you want it then and there?

Gifts and the Woman

"Whenever I give, I give myself."
—*Walt Whitman*

NICE SENTIMENT, Walt, but women need more, demand more. Women love tangible gifts. Even "nonmaterialistic" women often equate their desirability and men's feelings for them with the gifts given to them by their suitors. So, guys, you've got to give gifts other than just yourself.

From your—and her—perspective, a gift is great if it can be obtained with minimal effort (preferably one phone call), will not break your bank, and is perceived by her as a thoughtful, unique gesture. A tall order for any gift to measure up to, granted. But would I let you down? Sir, your month-by-month, occasion-by-occasion gift-giving guide awaits:

January

Martin Luther King Jr. Day. Just testing you. This is obviously not a gift-giving holiday. Use the occasion to show your thoughtful, progressive, giving-back-to-society side by discussing (a) the symbolic importance of the holiday and (b) where your relationship is going.

February

Valentine's Day. Ah, the first "major" of the year. Flowers are overused on this occasion and are therefore the worst bang for your buck. Go south, young man. Take your babe to Mexico or Jamaica for a three-day weekend. All-inclusive packages are very reasonably priced, even more so if you can get one from a discount travel clearance broker a week before departure. Add an element of surprise—tell her simply to clear her weekend and pack a bag. It's a thrilling touch. You ain't ever getting a better at bat, so you'd better score on this away game.

March

First Day of Spring. Now come the flowers. Have a great big, exotic spring bouquet delivered to her office. Her coworkers will notice, and she'll be all the more appreciative. Your card—"Every day with you is the first day of spring"—will leave nary a dry eye in the place.

April

Easter. Regardless of religion, everyone loves a good Easter egg hunt. Sure, get her candies (good ones, such as Godiva). But your special touch is setting up her very own egg hunt. Get some of those colorful plastic eggs and place notes inside them that signify personal services "coupons" that she can redeem with you. Try "this coupon entitles you to one great back rub," or "redeem this for a night of wining and dining at my house." You get the picture. Good for her and good for you.

May

Memorial Day. Get away from it all. Make reservations for a bed-and-breakfast weekend in the country. Sleep late, take afternoon walks, share the hammock, eat homemade cookies in bed. Everyone, absolutely everyone, is romantic at a great B & B.

June

By now it's been half a year since she got a great female consumer durable from you. She is in need of a major gift fix. Good ideas include a sterling silver picture frame (complete with a picture of the two of you) or, if you are feeling lucky, some fine silk lingerie.

July

Independence Day. Celebrate with a bang. Throw a party for her, because after all, she is your Miss America. Send out invitations to a few of your friends. Have a blowout barbecue, complete with fireworks. Guard against celebrating your "independence" too much.

August

Hmmm. The dog days of summer. Not a gift-giving excuse in sight—for the ordinary man, that is. Pick any random August day and just give her a gift. No fanfare, nothing fancy. How about a piece of sporting equipment that she's been wanting to use outdoors before the end of the great weather? And give it to her with a card that simply says, "Happy Friday." The understated nature of your gift giving only adds to your charm.

September

Birthday. We need to discuss her birthday sometime, so let's do it here. Her birthday is a big deal, and your gift had better be too. Don't sweat it, though. Get her a really, really nice watch. Your safest bet is to go to (or call) Tiffany's, ask the salesperson for help, and pick something out. If you happen to be off target, she can return it and select a watch she really loves. In any case, that trademark blue box will carry the day.

October

Halloween. Why not go shopping for fall clothes together? There is bound to be some item she wants but declines to buy (your clue is when you hear, "I've bought too many things already," or "I really like it, but it's a little expensive"). That's when you swoop in and buy it for her. Spontaneous, easy. And you know she likes it. What more could you ask for?

November

This is the month the gift-giving pros know to take off. You don't want to dilute your big splash next month.

December

Christmas/Hanukkah. The coup de grace of the gift-giving season. No clothes, as her tastes will be hard to peg. Nothing practical, as this is the season of magic. Go classic, go big. Go jewelry—and make it the real stuff. Diamond stud earrings, pearl choker, gold bangle bracelet, diamond solitaire necklace. It'll cost you—anywhere between $1,500 and $3,000, depending on quality—so, you may want to go this route only if you think she could be *the* girl (or at least, the girl for a while).

How to Buy a Diamond

"A thing is worth whatever
the buyer will pay for it."

—*Publilius Syrus*

DIAMONDS ARE A girl's best friend . . . but are they yours? They can be. One thing is certain: all proposals for marriage are most classically romantic (and have the best chance of succeeding) when done on one knee and accompanied by the right diamond engagement ring.

Sure, a diamond is the earth's most precious gemstone. Sure, it's going to sit on your beloved's finger for the rest of her life. But does it have to cost *soooo* much quid? And how do you know if what you're getting is worth what you're paying? Your summary guide to buying a diamond without losing your shirt follows.

Regardless of its style—round, marquise, emerald, pear, oval, or heart—the *value* of a diamond is determined by the four Cs: cut, clarity, color, and carat.

Cut is the most important of the four value variables. "Hey, that really sparkles" is the comment you are looking for. Cut determines the sparkle, the fire, the brilliance of a diamond. The problem is, cut is difficult for the purchaser to evaluate. Unlike the other three variables, no grading system exists for cut, and most diamonds are sized to maximize carat weight (and hence cost to you, Mr. Ego-needs-a-big-ring), sacrificing cut.

What to do? Get a jeweler's recommendation. Like a boxer, you need a good cut man in your corner. If your boss or parents have happily used someone for years, give him a shot. Find a jeweler you trust, and seek his counsel. And in the end, trust your own eye. Match the good taste you had in selecting your wife-to-be and you will do just fine.

Clarity is the amount of inclusions, or blemishes, in the diamond. The greater the number and size of inclusions, the lesser the grade of clarity. Clarity is a determining factor (although not as much as cut) in brilliance. A grade of FL means the diamond is flawless and you can't afford it (or even afford to insure it). A grade of IF designates the diamond as internally flawless, still not the right category for you unless you're spending significant inherited wealth. A grade of VVS1 or VVS2 means the diamond has very, very small inclusions, and VS1 or VS2 means the diamond has very small inclusions. These are your sweet spots! All four grades provide outstanding clarity. Select the right price point for you within this range. Stones with a grade of VS2 or better will not have any blemishes that are visible to the naked eye.

The last main segment of clarity grades, SI, is not really acceptable for a main stone. It is really best suited for use in necklaces or earrings in which lack of brilliance is not as noticeable.

Color is best when it is not there. The most valuable diamonds are those that approach colorlessness. Color is graded from D (colorless) to Z (most yellow), with the majority of engagement-grade diamonds in the color grades of F, G, H, I, and J. To the untrained eye, most diamonds will look white. To get the best feel for your desired color-price trade-off, place several next to each other. Color is a big driver of value (and therefore cost), yet most people respond more to the brilliance. So, unless you can get the best on all counts, go for what the ladies like—sparkle over color.

Don't waste your potential sports car money on great color if you or your fiancée desires a gold setting. Diamonds separated by one or two color grades will appear very similar in color when set in gold. If gold, go H, I, J. If platinum, go F, G, H. In general, spend the extra money on size or cut.

Carat is the standard measure of diamond size. Remember, size is of little value without reasonable cut, clarity, and color. A big, ugly diamond will impress only the unimpressive. Hardly your target audience. All things being equal, however, bigger is better. A good-quality big diamond says Mr. Wonderful, Mr. Successful, Mr. Right. Good messages to her, her family, her friends. A good-quality big diamond is also the best deterrent to advances from other suitors, pre- and postnuptials. Other men generally believe that such a rock can come from only a powerful, well-connected man (yes, you!) who should not be tangled with.

It is best to save the size consideration for last. Buy the biggest stone you can afford once you have selected the ranges of the other three criteria that make you the most comfortable. Most engagement ring stones are around 1 carat. A premium, in addition to the increase in price due to increase in carat weight, kicks in every time you hit one of the meaningful 0.5 carat barriers. That is, a diamond that is 1.55 carats will be more than 0.1 carat more expensive than a 1.45-carat diamond. The advice? Look to buy the carat weights just under the benchmarks—buy 0.9-, 1.4-, and 1.9-carat-weight diamonds. They will look as big as their just-bigger sister diamonds at a much better price. Moreover, diamonds with carat weights just under a 0.5 benchmark tend to have a better cut because the cut was not sacrificed to make the benchmark.

How much should a diamond ring set you back? The rule of thumb is that you should budget two months' *gross* salary (not your net, or take-home pay, but the *gross* pay) for an engagement ring and for a ten-year anniversary ring (hopefully your two months will give you a lot more at ten years—if not, see the "Business Life" section) and one month's gross salary for other important diamond gifts (for example, a diamond pendant for the birth of your first baby or diamond stud earrings for her thirtieth birthday). If you are like most men, you will look back and wish that you had spent as much as you could possibly afford. Make sure the ring speaks for you now and for the success you anticipate. You are *the man*—make sure your diamond looks like it.

How to Break It Off Like a Gentleman

"Marriage is a great institution,
but I'm not ready for an institution."

—*Mae West*

IT'S OVER. You know it. The problem is, she doesn't. The handling of this situation separates gentlemen from jerks. When it's properly handled, you'll feel OK, your ex-beloved will feel OK, and your reputation among the dating sisterhood will be unblemished (and perhaps enhanced). So, now that you've lost that loving feeling, how should you properly get this relationship behind you?

Gentleman's Rule #1:
Do it in person.

Any in-person breakup carries more weight. It shows you cared enough to make this final effort. It demonstrates you're man enough to take the yelling, crying, or yelling and crying, as the case may be. The in-person breakup also allows you to read you ex's body language and adapt the communication as necessary to make your point with minimum pain. Even if your relationship was primarily through long-distance calls or cyberspace, the in-person breakup is a sign of class.

Gentleman's Rule #2: Be direct.

Breakups call for being fair (painful but clear) rather than being nice (tender but dishonest). You must say, "It's over." Your ex-one-true-love can begin to get over you only once she internalizes that this is really it. If you do it right the first time, it saves both of you the pain of doing it again, and again, and again.

Gentleman's Rule #3:
Don't go halfway.

If you're going to do it, do it. Don't be a wimp and leave the door open for a possible reunion or "friendship." If either of you really *needs* another friend, it is always best to find someone other than each other. Post-breakup conjugal company—however tempting—confuses the issues and generally results in one of you feeling used.

Gentleman's Rule #4: Just say no.

Women often think they can change us. Your ex may think you are going through a phase and just need some time and space. You must not take the bait in whatever form—meeting mutual friends for a drink, a needed date to a work social event, or a casual movie matinee. The most manly "no" is one that is stated positively. Try saying, "It would be easy to say yes, but that would not be the fair thing to either of us."

Part II

Dining and Drinking

Smoothly Selecting a Wine

"Who does not love wine, women, and song
Remains a fool his whole life long."

—*Johann Heinrich Voss*

IN TODAY'S WORLD, a man must appear to know wine in both business and personal entertainment settings. The man who selects the wine is the de facto leader. At a business dinner, the man who can order and taste the wine skillfully and subtly is halfway down the road to getting a yes on his pitch. In intimate settings, a woman desires a man who can execute the last remaining vestiges of hunting and gathering. Since you can't kill, skin, and stuff a wild boar or harvest, stomp, and ferment grapes before her very eyes, it is critical to your manhood that you select the wine to accompany her meal.

How do you match food and wine?

The science of the choice dictates that the wine color match the color of the main dish. If the meal is on the lighter side—such as chicken, fish, or cream pasta—choose a white wine. If the meal is on the darker side—such as beef or tomato pasta—choose a red wine. But rules are meant to be broken. Often considerations such as the season (white in warm months, red in cooler) or the mood of the occasion (red is deeper, more robust, while white is peppier, more festive) will aid the selection.

How do you know if you are ordering a good wine?

The pros spend years accumulating a tasting base of knowledge. You, on the other hand, need follow only two simple rules.

First, order a reasonably expensive bottle, considering your budget and the occasion. Although there are many budget-priced wines, the odds of picking a *good* wine increase as the price increases. Second, ask your waiter (or the wine steward or sommelier as he is fancifully called) for a recommendation. He will be helpful in narrowing down that unwieldy list to a few sound choices.

To cork or not to cork?

Ahhh, that *is* the question. To experts, the cork can reveal certain things that may assist them in evaluating the wine. For the general public, the cork plays no part in the tasting ritual. If the waiter forces the cork upon you, confidently set it down next to your wineglass and begin tasting as instructed here.

The Taste

The wine arrives at your table. Your heart starts racing. Relax and read on. The art of wine tasting can be broken down into three Ss: swirling, sniffing, and sipping.

Swirl

Gently move the glass in a circular motion so that the wine comes halfway up the side of the glass. Continue this motion for about five seconds (this will seem frighteningly long until you are comfortable with your newfound expertise). Swirling increases the oxygen exposure to certain molecules in the wine, initiating a chemical reaction. The chemical reaction releases the aroma so it can be sniffed.

Sniff

Lift the rim of the glass to your nose and inhale deeply (yet quietly). You will not smell anything but wine. With practice,

Proper Pronunciation Is the First Step to Apparent Expertise

Cabernet sauvignon	cah-bear-nay so-ven-YAWN
Chablis	sha-BLEE
Chardonnay	shar-don-NAY
Chenin blanc	shen-nen BLAWNK
Merlot	mer-LOW
Pinot noir	PEE-no-n'wahr

you will get more accustomed to your smelling sense and will be able to sniff the nuances of the wine such as fruity, spicy, or flowery. The goal is to be able to evaluate the appropriate balance of those nuances.

Sip

This is where you can be easily exposed as a novice. Take a medium-size sip in your mouth and introduce the wine to your taste buds for a few seconds before swallowing. Do not dribble. Maintain a pleasant, yet serious and inquisitive expression. At this point, experts will take up to a minute to evaluate the wine against all the similar wine they have tasted as well as their expectations for the wine at hand. You will simply ask yourself, "Do I like it?" Trust your instincts.

Best Bets

Celebrating on a budget? Here are five great wines, each at about $10:

- Villa Mt. Eden Chardonnay, White California, 1995.

- Beaulieu Vineyard Cabernet, Red California, 1993.

- Ferrari-Carano Fume Blanc, White California, 1995.

- Cetamura Chianti, Badiua Coltibuno, 1995.

- Estancia Cabernet Sauvignon, Red California, 1994.

If money is no object, treat your taste buds to one of these fine selections:

- Chateau Petrus, Red Bordeaux, 1989 or 1990 (about $750 a bottle)

- Domaine Comtes Lefron Le Montrachet, White Burgundy, 1990 (about $500 a bottle)

- Beringer Napa Valley Reserve Chardonnay, California, 1994 or 1995 (about $35 a bottle)

How to Drink Like a Man

"The only way to get rid of a
temptation is to yield to it."
—*Oscar Wilde*

AGENT 007 HIT the martinis pretty hard, and yet he never appeared either shaken or stirred. What was his secret to drinking like a man? It's about drinking manly drinks, exercising manly drinking etiquette, and manhandling the hangover. Pour yourself a Scotch and water with a twist of lemon and read on.

Manly Drinks

Party punches, shots, and kegs are for boys. Microbeers and red wines are more manly. But the most manly drinks are those that are not enjoyed by the masses. Manly drinks make you the center of attention, unafraid to take charge. The next time everyone orders a beer, request a martini, or an upscale bourbon over ice. Watch the women swoon.

Martini (makes 2 drinks)

1. Pour 8 ounces of gin or vodka (fresh from the freezer) into a glass.

2. Add a capful or splash (no more than 1 ounce) of vermouth.

3. Stir slightly.

4. Add a twist of lemon or green olive to taste.

Manly Drinking Etiquette

There are times that are acceptable for getting drunk and times that are, to put it mildly, not. Experience often teaches which is which. One easy rule is that any event with work colleagues—whether a holiday party, a cocktail hour, or a charity dance—is off-limits to loading up. Work parties aren't fraternity parties—they are more about getting ahead than having fun. And women don't love a drunk as much as you think they do.

But, then again, there are times you'll *want* to get looped. When that time comes, your drinking decorum becomes more important as your intake increases. If you're going to be a drunk for a night, be a happy, considerate drunk for a night. Don't pick fights and don't miss the urinal. And don't even think about driving—and don't allow anyone you're with to drink and drive.

Manhandling the Hangover

In the grown-up world, the hangover has more repercussions than sleeping through your morning classes. Therefore, you need ways of quickly minimizing a hangover's debilitating effects. Your recommended six-step plan to self-renewal:

1. Drink a large glass of water before going to sleep.

2. Drink some coffee or a Diet Coke in the morning. The caffeine will stimulate your nervous system to get going again.

3. Get out of bed. Get the blood flowing and get your focus off how bad you feel.

4. Take a multivitamin. Your body needs all the replenishment it can get.

5. Eat something light, such as toast. It will help settle your stomach.

6. Take a steam bath. The warm steam opens your pores and helps you sweat out the alcohol.

Stocking Your Home Bar Like a Pro

"Too much of a good thing
can be wonderful."

—*Mae West*

WHETHER YOU ARE hosting a big blowout or a simple one-on-one, your home bar is a significant determinant to the success of the evening. Although alcohol is fattening, often results in terrible hangovers, makes you say stupid things, and can be an expensive habit, it is the straw that stirs the social event.

Once you get out of college, serving up alcohol at a party entails a little more than simply tapping the keg. Women expect more, your work colleagues expect more, even your buddies expect more.

The Well-Stocked Bar

This assortment and quantity is designed for a party of fifty people, give or take ten, depending on the lush level. Keep *each* item around in *lesser* quantities for smaller gatherings or the spontaneous event.

The Alcohol

Beer (3 six-packs import, 4 six-packs domestic,
5 six-packs light)

6 bottles merlot

12 bottles chardonnay (keep chilled)

6 bottles champagne (keep chilled)

2 fifths vodka (store in the freezer)

1 fifth gin

1   fifth rum

1   fifth whiskey

1   fifth Scotch

1   fifth Baileys

The Mixers

Club soda (5 two-liter bottles)

Tonic (5 two-liter bottles)

Sparkling water (10 one-liter bottles of Perrier)

Noncarbonated water (10 one-liter bottles of Evian)

Orange juice (4 gallons)

Cranberry juice (2 gallons)

Coke and Diet Coke (36 cans Diet Coke, 24 cans Coke—cans hold the fizz better than large bottles)

Lemons, limes, and oranges for slices and peels (6 lemons, 3 limes, 3 oranges)

Green olives (1 jar)

Maraschino cherries (1 jar)

Ice and more ice (10 bags for drinks, 5 bags for the cooler—*everyone* underestimates ice needs)

Brewed coffee (think ahead!)

The Hardware

Heavy-duty blender

Stainless shaker and stirring rods

Large ice bucket and ice tongs

Large punch bowl

Large cooler (for bottled beer and wine)

Small cutting surface, lemon peeler, and small knife

Corkscrew

Bottle opener

Swizzle sticks and drink picks

Coasters or cocktail napkins

Proper glasses, including a set of highballs, old-fashioneds, martini, wine, and champagne glasses

Your Bar Briefs

Go for brand names when stocking your bar. If necessary in a big bash, refill the top-shelf labels with the cheaper brands once everyone gets a good buzz going and can't taste the difference. As for wines and champagnes, buy an assortment in a moderate price range. Buy one excellent bottle of red, white, and champagne for that special late-night encounter.

A few final bar-stocking touches. Remember to provide beverage alternatives for nondrinkers. Consider a nonalcoholic punch blend or a sparkling apple cider. Don't skimp on mixers that will also be served straight. Also, consider offering a special party drink. No, not Jell-O shooters. A simple-to-make, adult, hip concoction, such as a pitcher of mimosas or martinis, will add festivity to your bar offerings.

Cocktail Parties Made Easy

"Strange to see how a good dinner and feasting reconciles everybody."

—*Samuel Pepys*

THE DINNER PARTY is an unnecessary nightmare. Too formal, too expensive. Leave it to the middle-aged socialites. Your party is the cocktail party—it swings. And it is flexible in terms of duration, dress, guest number and mix, food and drink offerings, and overall feel. A cocktail party is a novice's answer to all those invitations that a modern gentleman must repay.

Party Primer #1: The Guests

If your guests suck, your party will suck. There is no substitute for interesting and congenial guests. Try to put together a mix of party people—some from the same circles, some from different—that may enjoy talking with each other. Too many work colleagues, too many guys, too many of anything will be dull. Variety is the spice of a party.

Party Primer #2: The Host

That's you. The most successful parties are those in which the guests feel welcome and comfortable. Start by greeting *each* guest at the door, making him or her feel special. It's important to make meaningful introductions of one guest to another. Mingling is an art, and helping your entire party mingle is a real skill.

Party Primer #3: The Help

Hire it. You're an (almost) adult. It's your prerogative to hire people to help put on a great party. You will need a caterer to make the food, set the buffet, pass the hors d'oeuvres, clean up stray plates and glasses, and tend bar. A party of fifty can be handled by a staff of two. As you write the check, just keep saying, "I'm a general manager, not a line worker; I'm a general manager, not a line worker."

Party Primer #4: The Setting

Atmosphere is everything. Music should be planned in advance and cued on your multidisc CD player. Spin a good mix and keep the volume at a low level. Dim the lights, but not so much that the room resembles your eighth-grade make-out parties. Candles add an interesting glimmer, especially on the buffets and in the bathrooms. Have several flower arrangements delivered and place them where people are most likely to notice them, such as the front hall and on the buffet. Don't forget the power of smell: a natural log fire or potpourri simmering on the stove is nice. Make sure you or your caterers use attractive linens, plates, and glassware. Rent them, buy them, borrow them—you must have them.

Party Primer #5: The Drink

Thank you, sir; may I have another—see page 33.

Party Primer #6: The Food

Pretzel rods, BBQ chips, cookies . . . oops, that's the poker party. Tell your caterer what kind of things you like and would like to serve your guests. Ask for the caterer's suggestions as to what works well. Consider the following finger food feast:

Cold Honey-Baked Ham Slices

Petite Warm Medium-Rare Beef Tenderloin Sandwiches

Assorted Gourmet Cheese Tray (Gouda, Sharp Cheddar, and Brie)

Assorted Cold Vegetables and Dip (Carrots, Cucumbers, Celery, Baby Corns)

Spicy Olive Oil–Pasta Salad

Fresh Breads and Rolls

Fresh Mixed-Fruit Salad

A Sweet Tray of Brownies, Truffles, and—for a whimsical touch—Rice Krispies Squares

The Sixty-Minute Gentleman Gourmet

"The best number for a dinner party is two—myself and a head waiter."

—*Nubar Gulbenkian*

OUR GOAL HERE is *not* to make you into a gourmet—rather, it is to make you a gourmet for *one* night. A feast created by you, for her, puts your artistic and feminine side on display—in a manly way. Also, making her dinner gets her into your home in a relaxed setting, which is often half the battle.

You need only one make-her-a-great-meal trick in your bag. Practice the meal that follows a few times for your parents or friends before cooking it when it counts. It is not just the quality of the meal that matters in impressing her—it is the process of the cooking evening. Think of what you've liked when a woman has cooked for you—probably the appearance of effortlessness, the feeling of personal hospitality, and the aura of confidence.

Your one-night gourmet meal can be used over and over again for different dates. But in each case, try to use it in the right spot, thinking of it as the culinary closer. The meal outlined here is a wonderful balance of simplicity, richness, and likability. If you really know what you are doing, feel free to go off the board, but this offering is a tried-and-true pleaser.

The Entree—Mushroom Risotto

Risotto is an Italian dish in which short-grain rice is slowly simmered and constantly stirred in order to gradually absorb the liquid in which it is cooked, making for a creamy, hearty main dish. For your evening in, risotto shares the ease, versatility, and "everyone-loves-Italian" virtues of pasta but gives the punch and panache of a seldom-seen (and therefore, more impressive) dish.

Your Ingredients

7   cups canned beef broth

4   tablespoons olive oil

1   medium yellow onion, chopped

1   pound fresh sliced mushrooms

3   cups arborio (or similar) rice

1   cup white wine

Your Preparation

In a medium pot, bring broth to a boil. Reduce heat and simmer. In another pot, sauté onion and mushrooms in oil over low heat until soft (about 5 minutes). Add rice and cook another 3 minutes. Add 1 cup of the broth and stir until the rice absorbs it. Continue this process until about half the broth has been added to the rice and has been absorbed. Add wine. Add remaining broth 1 cup at a time until absorbed by the rice. Total cooking time is about 30 minutes. This dish is time sensitive, so pay attention.

Serve the risotto with salt and pepper to taste and grated Parmesan cheese at the table.

The Salad—Mixed Greens and Vinaigrette

When it comes to the salad, you can get as simple or as fancy as you like. Experiment. The following mixed green salad always works well. Make it ahead of time—before you start preparing the main course.

Your Ingredients

Bibb lettuce

Romaine lettuce

Watercress

Fresh spinach

Vinaigrette dressing (bottled is fine, but make it good)

Pine nuts (about ½ cup)

Gorgonzola or blue cheese, crumbled (about 2 ounces)

Your Preparation

Tear greens into bite-size pieces, rinse, and place in a large bowl. Add a small amount of dressing, tossing the salad to lightly coat the leaves. Throw in some pine nuts and cheese. Do not overdue it. Toss. Add pepper at table to taste.

The Accompaniments—Wine and Bread

Women, as a rule, love wine. Select an appropriate bottle to round out your masterpiece of a meal (see page 27). An equally important part of dinner is fresh bread. The best choice is a crunchy French baguette—a touch of European flair regularly available at your corner bakery or in the fresh bread section of your supermarket. Warm the bread prior to serving.

The Dessert—Fresh Berries and Cream

No meal is complete without dessert—even if one of you is dieting or is not really a dessert person. A universally popular finisher is fresh seasonal berries and cream. It is cosmopolitan, tasty, and a snap to prepare. Any type of berry will do—try a mix from any two of strawberries, blueberries, blackberries, or raspberries—with your choice of cream. Cream possibilities include anything from the fancy (crème anglaise) to the simple (purchased Cool Whip or fresh cream) and the fattening (gourmet vanilla ice cream).

How to Make an Omelette

"'Tis the part of a wise man not to . . .
venture all his eggs in one basket."

—*Cervantes*

THERE ARE TIMES when a woman's place is anywhere but the kitchen. You may want to impress her by whipping up breakfast after a passionate night together. Your babe may be sick, at work, or out of town. Or simply, you may be between women. In any and all such cases, the omelette is your food friend.

The omelette is the Deion Sanders of the culinary world—a multipurpose food weapon effective for breakfast, lunch, dinner, and late night. Follow these six easy steps and you're on your way to making a great omelette.

1. **Your tools:** a pan (the heavier the better, with low sides), a spatula or wooden spoon, a fork, and a mixing bowl.

2. **Let's begin.** For each serving, crack three eggs into the mixing bowl, picking out any errant shell pieces. Add about ¼ cup milk for each serving and mix with a fork until combined.

3. **Ingredients.** Select and chop desired ingredients to fill your omelette—cheese, cooked bacon or ham, bell pepper, tomato, and mushrooms all make fine choices. When you have chosen a combination of ingredients, name the upcoming omelette after yourself—a step that heightens the impressiveness of your culinary creation. (A Swiss and spinach is The Davis Omelette).

4. **Halftime!** You are now only five minutes away from eating, so get everything ready to accompany your

omelette, such as the morning newspaper, a single-stem rose in a vase, toast, ice water, and coffee.

5. **Cooking.** Warm the pan over medium-high heat a minute or so. Pour three spoonfuls of cooking oil or butter into the pan and heat for 1 minute. Add egg mixture. Use the wooden spoon or spatula to gently lift the omelette edge. After 2 minutes or so, sprinkle your selected fillings onto the egg. The total cooking time will be 3 to 4 minutes, depending on the heat and your desired moisture of the end product. Look for eggs to be done, but not dry.

6. **Finale.** Fold over with the spatula or spoon, and tip the pan to ease the omelette onto your waiting plate. Add salt and pepper to taste.

Take a bow and enjoy—Wolfgang Puck, watch out.

The Backyard Grill

"Simple cooking cannot be trusted
to a simple cook."

—*Countess Morphe*

HOT FUN IN the summer. The equipment, the flames, the sizzle, the hoopla of a backyard culinary celebration all say "man in charge—stand back and admire." Luckily, the grill is a forgiving instrument, and everything tastes better cooked on it. What group of buddies can resist steaks and beers in the sunny backyard? What woman can resist grilled tuna and chardonnay on your terrace in the early evening glow? Exactly.

Your Instruments

Forget the goofy gadgets you will never use. Here are the tools you want. Wield them with import and confidence.

Grill

Grill cleaning brush

All-purpose spatula (with a long wooden handle)

Skewers

Tongs (to help turn items)

Basting brushes

Hinged wire basket (for holding small or juicy vegetables)

Apron

Your Fire

Your fire building can be as simple as buying a bag of pre-lighter-fluid-soaked charcoal briquettes. Charcoal provides a steady, sure heat without much fuss. To ensure that there is no chemical taste, some cooks prefer to use kindling, rather than lighter fluid, to start the coals. For more exotic occasions try adding mesquite, hickory, or applewood chips. Herbs or spices—such as garlic, poppy seeds, or black pepper—can be sprinkled over coals or burning chips to further flavor your endeavor in a deep and interesting way that table seasoning can not.

The size of the fire depends on the amount and type of food being grilled. Always begin with the charcoal in a pyramid, extending as far as the grill rack space you will need. Allow the fire to burn thirty minutes—the coals should be glowing red in part and light gray ash in part—before cooking. When cooking items that need direct heat—such as vegetables, steaks, burgers, and fish fillets—spread the coals into an even patch about two deep. When cooking items that need indirect heat—such as ribs, game birds, and whole fish—push the coals away from the center of the grill and cook inside the ring of fire.

Your "Special Sauce"

The easiest way to impress, as well as express your creativity at the grill, is to add a "special sauce" to the food. This act—known as marinating—can be done beforehand or while the meal is on the grill. Never reveal the recipe for your special sauce. Mystery enhances the palate. Try the following to spruce up the most basic grill:

- **Herbed butter.** A slice of herbed butter on a sizzling steak or burger is a simple masterpiece. To make herbed butter, combine ½ cup unsalted butter, 2 tablespoons dried cilantro or sage, 2 tablespoons chopped green onion, and several shakes of salt and pepper. Beat until smooth, form the mixture into a log, wrap in plastic, refrigerate until firm, and then slice.

- **Citrus marinade.** A citrus marinade is a light, flavorful complement to many chicken or fish dishes. It is best to soak the chicken or fish for 1 to 2 hours in the sauce before grilling. A satisfactory alternative is to brush on the marinade throughout the grilling process. To make citrus marinade, mix together ½ cup olive oil, ¼ cup lemon juice, ¼ cup chopped green onion, 1 tablespoon dried tarragon or dill, 1 teaspoon pepper, and several shakes of salt.

Your Technique

1. Brush the grill rack with olive oil, or spray with a nonstick primer such as *Pam*, before using to prevent foods from sticking.

2. If time is of the essence or multiple items must be juggled on the grill, cook food about halfway in the oven or on the stove and finish up on the grill.

3. If a fire flares up, move the food away and let the fire burn off. Dousing flare-ups with water results in an uneven coal burn.

4. Remove food from the grill just before it's fully cooked, as the food will continue to cook a bit off the fire.

5. Know your grill. Practice. Nothing sticks in the craw like an undercooked meal.

Your Food

Wonderful grilling recipes can be found in any cookbook. Some suggestions to consider are:

- For chicken and poultry, try whole quail, squab, or Cornish game hens, in addition to the always-good chicken quarters (with a teriyaki, honey mustard, or hickory barbecue sauce).

- For beef and lamb, try pepper flank steak, beef tenderloin kabob, lamb chops, or zesty barbecued baby back ribs, in addition to the ever reliable New York Strip, Filet Mignon, or ¾-pound hamburger.

- For fish, try whole trout or snapper au papillote, tuna steak, or scallop and shrimp kabob.

- For vegetables, try red potatoes, corn in the husk, or portobello mushrooms, in addition to the classic vegetable kabob.

Your Cleaning Ritual

After each grilling, brush your grill rack with a brass brush. Every few times, remove the cold ashes and other debris from the bottom of the grill. Clean the inside and outside of the grill as necessary, usually a couple of times per season.

Spotting and Smoking That Fine Cigar

"Happiness? A good cigar, a good meal,
another good cigar, and a good
woman—or a bad woman; it depends on
how much you can handle."

—*George Burns*

WINSTON CHURCHILL—statesman. Red Auerbach—winner. Arnold Schwarzenegger—macho, self-made success. George Burns—laughter and longevity. Demi Moore—stylish, sexy. All cigar smokers. All connoisseurs of the timeless tobacco that can say it all.

What a cigar says loudest is enjoyment. A great cigar can uniquely and wonderfully cap a summer's best golf round, a big business deal closing, a winning evening of poker, or a fine dinner with friends or colleagues

Cigars are constructed of three parts: wrapper, binder, and filler. The wrapper is the outside leaf, it dictates appearance. The binder holds the cigar together. The filler—both the type of tobacco leaf used and how it is rolled—determines the taste and smokability. The best cigars are hand-rolled.

The two biggest variables in cigars are size and color.

In cigars, size *does* matter. Larger is not necessarily better—just different. Although cigars come in all lengths (generally five to nine inches long) it is the girth of the cigar that is the important taste variable. The girth of a cigar, known as the ring gauge, is measured in increments of $\frac{1}{64}$ inch, so a cigar with a ring gauge of 42 is $\frac{42}{64}$-inch thick. The larger the ring gauge, the fuller and smoother the cigar (the largest readily available cigar is a 64 ring gauge, or 1-inch round). The smaller ring gauges, say 30 to 35, make for a lighter, more quickly burning smoke.

As with wines, the darker the cigar, the more full-bodied it will be. Darker cigars tend to be more aromatic and flavorful, like a deep red wine. You can therefore determine an appropriate smoke for an event by matching its color intensity to that of the anticipated wine.

How to Light Up

Cut or bite a level piece about a quarter inch long off the smoking end of cigar. Holding the cigar horizontal to the ground, use a match or lighter to make contact with end, slightly charring it evenly. Now put the cigar to your lips, holding the flame a minute fraction from the end, and inhale deeply. Slightly rotate the cigar while inhaling to ensure that it remains evenly lit. Gently blow on the lit end to facilitate its burn.

Storing the Goods

A stale cigar is a bad cigar. Here are a few tips to ensure tasty tobacco:

- Purchase cigars from a cigar shop that has excellent storage facilities. Smoke, or properly store, cigars within three days of purchase.

- A humidor—a specially made cedar box that controls humidity—can keep cigars fresh for years.

- In the absence of a personal humidor (cost: about $300 to $500), place cigars in an airtight bag in the vegetable crisper section of a refrigerator. Place several drops of water in the bag (away from the cigars!) every few days. This will keep the cigars reasonably fresh for a month or so.

Best Bets

Smoking on a budget? Here are three great cigars for under $2 each:

- Montesino Gran Corona
- Punch No. 75
- Cuesta-Rey Cabinet No. 95

When money is no object, try one of these fine selections:

- Fuente Opus X Robusto (about $20)
- Davidoff Double "R" (about $18)
- Arturo Fuente Don Carlos Robuston (about $12)

Part III

Business
Life

Getting a Good Job Even in Tough Times

"I have nothing to offer but blood,
toil, tears and sweat."

—*Winston Churchill*

To WORK OR not to work, that is *not* the question. You gotta do it. Even "aspiring" actors are waiters while they're aspiring. The questions are—what field are you going to work in, which job are you going to do, where are you going to do it, and for whom?

Regardless of your job, you will likely spend about 70 percent of your waking life working. Add in the time commuting to work, social functions related to work, and when you can't get work off your mind, and the percentage of your life spent working is even higher. Yes, this employment stuff is one of the biggest influences on your life. To get a great job (even in tough times), stuff these time-tested words of advice into your briefcase along with your résumé:

Seek and ye shall find.

In just the last ten years, the manner in which employers seek potential new employees has dramatically changed. More than half of the new jobs available today are with small companies. These companies often do not have the sophisticated hiring infrastructures that the big employers of old did. What is the result of this tectonic shift in employer hiring behavior? Potential employees must be aggressive in their job search.

Job seekers tend to overuse two channels that are relatively ineffective. The vast majority of jobs are *not* filled through classified help-wanted ads, so don't spend a lot of time there.

And people almost never get a job by sending a blind résumé, so forget that. Rather, be proactive in your search as outlined in the following tips.

Waste not, want not. Not.

Ah, not true when it comes to seeking a new job. A job seeker must spend countless hours chasing opportunities, and it is likely that more than 90 percent of those hours will turn out to have been wasted. The problem is, it is impossible to tell in advance which exact hours will be the ones that make it all worth the effort.

Try the following three-step approach and you'll be on your way to landing the right job.

First, think about the types of things in which you are interested. Make a list of the fields (not companies or jobs) that are likely to be a good match for your career interests. Think about what types of areas would hold your attention for ten years—Technology? Wall Street? Entertainment?

Second, research the best companies in your field of interest. Who offers the most responsibility to younger employees? Who usually promotes from within? Who offers the most collegial or flexible work environment? Who has the best record with respect to minority advancement or social responsibility? Who offers stock-option participation to all levels of employees? It is best to approach all the companies that might fit the bill, ruling out the less desirable ones only when you get offers from the more desirable ones.

Third, plan your attack to get an interview. This begins with constructing a résumé (a task so important it has its own section—see page 57). Next, determine the appropriate contact person at each firm. Avoid the human resources department at all costs. Use whatever contacts you have to get in front of the right person's face. Do you know someone at your target employer that can help make sure your résumé gets a looking at? If not, do you know someone who knows someone? It is often *who* you know, not what you know, that gets your foot in the door.

Never let 'em see you sweat.

When it comes to the interview, you're judged by outward signs. Obviously, your appearance, demeanor, and rapport in the interview is just about everything when you get to that point in the hiring process. The interview also demands, and is granted, its own section of this book—see page 66.

Sticks and stones may break my bones . . .

But in the job hunting game, words (and the lack thereof) must never hurt you. You must be able to accept and handle rejection. Many people claim that the three keys to getting a job are persistence, persistence, persistence. Fax your résumé to the appropriate contact person and follow up with a phone call a week later. If you don't get a return call, send a friendly E-mail message or call again in three to five days. Still no word? Try to reach another entry point in the company, one who can find out if the company is hiring in your area of interest. You will face rejection many times in your employment search. Do not ever give up—you only need *one* yes.

A rolling stone gathers no moss.

A good time to look for a job is when you already have one. The best time to explore new opportunities is when you are happy in your current job. A typical job search lasts six months for entry-level jobs and nine to twelve months for middle- or senior-level jobs. Factor in more time to find the job that is just what you are looking for.

The wheel that squeaks the loudest is the one that gets the grease.

No matter how much you like the offer, it often comes down to the money. After you have received an offer that is attractive, but needs to be more financially rewarding, you must tactfully negotiate.

1. **Know the market.** Find out the market rate for the type of position you're going after.

2. **Plan your pitch.** Practice what you are going to say, and prepare answers to anticipated objections. Be direct and don't ramble.

3. **Check the flip side.** Look at it from their side to make sure your demands are realistic.

4. **Be specific.** You must counter with a specific number. Think 15 percent above their offer.

5. **Try for spiffs.** Perhaps you can get noncash benefits thrown in, such as stock options, participation in a bonus pool, a company-paid laptop PC or cell phone, or more vacation time.

6. **Be diplomatic.** Remember, they have the power and must choose to *give* it to you.

7. **Remember that it's not all about the money.** Early in your career a larger salary is not nearly as important as the learning, contacts, and responsibility of the job you're being offered.

Building a Top Résumé

"Anyone can win—unless there is a second entry."
—*George Ade*

THE RÉSUMÉ IS the first step in selling yourself. Look at your résumé and ask yourself: does it reflect you and your skills in a clear and compelling fashion? Employers screening your résumé will decide, in less time than it took you to print the thing out, whether to grant you an interview. It's your job to make sure your résumé catches their attention.

Understand, though, that no résumé—even one that brands you a varsity-letter-winning, Rhodes Scholar–traveling, under-privileged-kid-counseling, shut-in-food-delivering, summa cum laude J.D./M.D./M.B.A. graduate—gets you a job. A résumé can only persuade a potential employer to give you a chance to *interview* for a job. Think of it as a tool to get your foot in the door.

Look to the following pointers to separate your résumé from the pack.

1. **Obey the one-page rule.** Regardless of how many skills, honors, and accomplishments you think you have, your résumé must *never* exceed one page. A prospective employer will give your résumé no more than fifteen seconds, so you must aggressively self-edit to ensure that your most distinguishing accomplishments jump off the page. Besides, any more than one page will show that you lack the conciseness important in the work world. Keep in mind that some tricks to getting more on your allotted page (such as providing references on a separate sheet later) are acceptable and some tricks are not (such as using smaller than 10-point type or less than normal margins).

2. **Include what's relevant; omit what isn't.** All résumés should include the following:

   - Your name, home address, contact phone number, and, if available, fax and E-mail

   - A record of your college and graduate school degrees, and years

   - Selected academic honors and awards

   - A record of your employment history, with job titles and years

   - A brief summary of responsibilities, accomplishments, and attained skills at each post

   - Professional training and affiliations

   - Relevant licenses and accreditation

   - Knowledge of foreign languages and other relevant atypical skills

   - Professional and civic honors or leadership posts

   It is best not to include the following:

   - Past salary information or current salary requirements

   - References to age, religion, race, or political affiliations

   - Hobbies (unless your hobby makes you more attractive—i.e., better qualified for the position)

   - Any attachments such as "deal summaries" or "fact sheets"

3. **Put your best foot forward.** If your academic credentials are very impressive and you are within five years out of school, lead with your education

summary. If your recent jobs and accomplishments make you strongly qualified for the job, lead with your employment history. In either case, use active verbs to bring your experiences to life—words such as *led, developed, designed, sold, built, reduced, delivered, negotiated,* or *organized.*

4. **One size does not fit all.** Customize your résumé to suit each potential job. Each position you apply for demands a unique slant on the qualifications your résumé highlights. It may be different skills, such as finance for one job, marketing for another. Or it may be your Chicago education if you are applying for a Chicago-based job. Don't be afraid to drop some otherwise important stuff that may not be as impressive to a particular potential employer if you can use the space to add stuff that will get that employer's attention.

5. **Keep the presentation clear and strong.** Use good paper (generally 50 percent cotton/50 percent linen) in a basic white or light cream. Standard fonts, such as Times Roman are best. Think through the best use of bullet points, underlining, and indentation for emphasis and ease of reading. Use as few words as possible to make your point. Double- and triple-check grammar and spelling, and have at least two other people read and critique the readability of your résumé.

6. **Seek professional help.** Advice and models are available—for free or for a fee. Review résumé books for helpful hints. Review résumés of colleagues who've gotten good jobs. If necessary, hire a résumé consultant or an employment advisory service to help you out. Don't be afraid to have the best résumé you can. And make a habit out of updating your résumé every year to help remind you to actively guide your career.

Networking—Getting Close to Those Who Can Help You

"Knowledge is power, if you know the right person."

—*Ethel Watts Mumford*

WHAT DO A bank heist and landing a great opportunity have in common? About 80 percent of both are inside jobs. Opportunities come to those in the know—those who know a job is available, who know the contact point for getting a foot in the door, and often, who know the person who is making the hiring decision.

A satire posted on the Internet—"The Six Degrees of Separation of Kevin Bacon"—explores the notion that no more than six films separate any actor from a film in which the actor Kevin Bacon has appeared. Funny, yes—telling, you bet. Do you know someone (1) who knows someone, (2) who knows someone, (3) who knows someone, (4) who knows someone, (5) who knows someone, (6) who knows the person you are looking to get in contact with? Those who master networking—the art of establishing a powerful web of personal connections—are often much *less* than six degrees of separation away from the person who can provide the big opportunity, the big break. Make networking an important "to do" each week. In today's business world, you need to be both good *and* connected.

Do *not* buy into the following four networking myths when trying to get ahead.

Myth #1: Good things come to those who wait.

Ever since The Book said that the meek shall inherit the earth, people have hidden behind this and similar phrases to justify lack of ambition. The fact is, it is impossible to get ahead unless you have the goal of getting ahead and are willing to pay the price to attain that goal. Success—fame, fortune, an interesting work life—rarely just knocks on your front door.

Dreams become goals when you write them down. Try it. What do you want to do that you're not doing? Lay out a plan to get there. Specifically, include people who are doing what you want to do and who might help you get there. Creating a solid plan is the first step. Aggressively taking action to realize it is the second step.

Myth #2: The world is a giant meritocracy, in which the best candidate gets the job.

No such thing. More often than not, employers hire people they know, or who are known by people they know. Previous contact is a way that potential employers get comfortable that a candidate is the right person for the opportunity in terms of skills and personality. And never underestimate the fact that people like to work with people who they like.

Myth #3: Big breaks in business are due to luck.

Bull. People make their own luck. Luck can be manufactured from hard work in the office, hard work improving skills, and hard work networking.

It is critical to focus as much time building your network as doing your job. A career needs only a few breaks. The best jobs are those that provide a platform to come into contact with senior people inside and outside your organization—people who can do something for you if they like you and your work. Don't make the mistake of spending the majority of your time impressing those who can't help you get what you want. Early in your work life, try to align yourself with an organization that is respected and known in the community and your field of interest in order to provide you a more credible profile beyond your own name as you network.

Myth #4: Only those born into wealth have great contacts.

True, contacts, like money, can be inherited. But contacts, like money, are most often earned. Follow these nine networking habits, and you and your descendants will have more contacts than you know what to do with.

Nine Nifty Networking Habits

1. Introduce yourself whenever possible to those who expand your circle. Don't let a function go by without identifying and pursuing the important introductions.

2. Volunteer on professional, civic, and charitable organizations. Attend business and social functions. Join a couple of respected clubs. You can't network from inside your apartment.

3. Stay in contact with those who move on from your circles, whether they are colleagues from the fraternity, graduate school, or your company.

4. Always reintroduce yourself in follow-up contacts. "Mr. X, it's great to see you again. I'm Donn Davis from World Media. Your company has made some smart acquisitions since I saw you at the Chicago Food Depository Black Tie last winter." Your networking target will, of course, have forgotten you and will respect you for saving him or her the embarrassment. Always be brief—fifteen seconds or less.

5. To get your foot in the door, look to meet for career advice. It's a way to make a contact and to impress on a no-pressure basis. Most people like to offer advice and will like you just for listening attentively.

6. Attend conferences in your field of interest. The conference setting usually allows time specifically for networking.

7. Many of the best new job opportunities come from clients or others with whom you come in contact in your current job. Always be on your best business behavior.

8. Contacts that aren't nurtured go stale. Look for follow-up contact opportunities for people you do meet, such as news items that may be of interest, holiday cards, and brief hellos when you run across them again.

9. Be bold. Be persistent.

How to Work a Room

"Conversation is not a search after knowledge, but an endeavor at effect."

—*John Keats*

To MOST SUCCESSFULLY network your way nearer to the top, you must learn how to "work a room." To successfully work a room you must make a good impression with as many people as possible in as little time as possible. Try these tips at your next economic club luncheon or charity black-tie gala.

- **Keep moving.** Your goal is to shake hands, exchange a personal pleasant comment, and smile as you gracefully move to the next group. People generally understand that people need to meet lots of people and can't stay and chat.

- **Remember names.** People are flattered when you remember their name (and even the name of their spouse) prior to being reintroduced. Before an event, go over the attendee list and refresh yourself as to whom you might run into.

- **Love the one you're with.** Give the person you are talking with your undivided attention. Make the individual feel that you really care about the conversation. Compliment the person, talk about him or her. Do not look over your shoulder at the rest of the party. Two minutes of laser-focused, personal chatter goes a long way.

- **Don't forget the little people.** People have a tendency to talk only to those at their same level or above in the power structure. Be sure to spend time with selective underlings, including administrative assistants and people new to the organization. You can learn many things from these people—things that those removed from the trenches don't know. And having a reputation as being a man of the people will serve you well.

- **Take the initiative.** People are almost never offended, and are often flattered, when someone takes the initiative to approach them. Just walk up and introduce yourself. You will be more efficient and effective by being assertive.

- **Circle back to the most important contacts on your way out.** Pick the people with whom you want to reinforce your presence, and make another contact with them on your way out. It takes only ten minutes or so to make the exit rounds with twenty people. Last impressions are the most memorable.

How to Interview Well

"Eighty percent of success is showing up."
—*Woody Allen*

A RÉSUMÉ IS like an NCAA Basketball Tournament bid—it only gets you into the game. Similar to March Madness, you will be up against others in rounds of single elimination—in the work world those rounds are called interviews. In college hoops, it is rare that the best team on paper (your résumé) wins. The tournament champion (who gets the job) is determined by how well the team plays (how well you interview).

So, think of preparing to interview well just as you would think of preparing for the big title game. Although certain people have more natural talent at interviewing—just as some players have more natural ability than others—research, practice, and coaching can make anyone better.

Here are seven keys to help you rise to the top of your interview game.

1. **Master time management**. Be early by fifteen minutes or so. Allow for getting lost, late trains, no cabs, inadequate parking, and other juvenile-seeming excuses that, when offered, are worse than being late itself. Being early allows you to acclimate to the surroundings, freshen up in a rest room, and mentally prepare. Also, the interviewer may want to start a few minutes early and will remember you fondly for being available. If you have more than one meeting to attend, make sure to schedule appointments far enough apart to allow for your interviewer's running late or wanting to spend more time (a good sign!) with you.

2. **Get assistants on your side.** Whoever else you talk to—a secretary, an administrative assistant, the human resources manager, or a department subordinate—is likely to be part of the screening process. You need to get these people on your side. Ask their name when you call or meet, and make a note to address them by name in subsequent contacts. These intermediaries have more influence than you think.

3. **Look the part**. Appearance counts. The adage about first impressions is magnified to the max in job interviews. Most interviewers will make up their mind about you in the first five minutes. A big part of this is how you look. Always wear a suit and tie, even if the company culture or potential job does not demand it. Stick to the basics: navy or gray solid suit, white shirt, and conservative power tie (see "Suit Yourself," page 117). Don't wear jewelry, other than a watch. Pay careful attention to good grooming: a close shave, short clean nails, and a smart haircut. If you don't look the part, you won't get the job.

4. **Make sure your greeting reflects your professionalism.** Look alert but at ease. Make sure your handshake is firm. Maintain eye contact at all times—that is your first step to establishing rapport. Keep a formal posture and demeanor, but act like a pro ready for much bigger challenges than the interview. Always make sure the interviewer feels that he or she is running the show; it's your job to show your potential new employer what a loyal disciple you are.

5. **Get a conversation going**. The best interviews are conversations, not stilted exchanges of questions and answers. The goal is a fifty-fifty division of talking between the interviewer and you. If the person enjoys talking with you, he or she may enjoy working with

you. People tend to hire people they like. It is critical that you keep your answers focused and organized. Don't be overly curt, but follow a rule of thumb that no answer should exceed thirty seconds without facilitating the interviewer's involvement—nobody can pay attention longer than that, so the only impression you can leave is that of a bore.

6. **Don't interview the interviewer**. You are the one under the microscope, not the interviewer or the potential employer. The only appropriate questions for you to ask are about responsibility and opportunities for advancement. Your job is to sell you, and you can do that only by keeping the focus of the conversation on your accomplishments, your skills, and your interest in the job. Save all other questions—benefits, salary, title, drug test policy—for much later in the process, preferably *after* you have an offer. You don't want to give your potential employer reasons not to hire you.

7. **Have answers to the top ten interview questions**. If you knew most of the questions to a test in advance, wouldn't you figure out the answers beforehand? Think through your best answer to each of the ten most frequently asked interview questions. Don't script out your comments in detail, but rather think of the two or three points you want to make in response to each question. Your goal is to sound smart without sounding canned. Always have positive answers to these questions—especially when asked about your current employer:

- Why are you interested in this job?

- Why are you willing to leave your current job?

- What are your unique qualifications for this job?

- What are your greatest strengths?

- What are your greatest weaknesses?

- What do you enjoy doing outside of work?

- How do you approach long periods of hard work?

- What can you tell me about the last new skills you learned?

- How would you relate some of your past experiences to this opportunity?

- Is there anything else about yourself you would like me to know?

Making an Effective Speech

"The human brain starts working the
moment you are born and never stops until
you stand up to speak in public."

—*Sir George Jessel*

AT SOME TIME, everyone is called on to make a speech. At some
time, everyone is apprehensive about making that speech. You
know it is an honor—it just is hard to embrace the honor with
pure delight. When it is your turn to step up to the podium,
keep in mind the following suggestions.

A great beginning is critical.

In the first minute, you will either hook the audience or lose
them to their dessert and thoughts of all the things they could
be doing other than listening to you. As Roy Orben said: "You
can't go wrong if you think of the first two minutes of your
speech as an audition. It's a 120-second sample that has to con-
vince your listeners that the remaining twenty minutes are
worth their time and attention." Although there is no set for-
mula for beginning a speech, memorable introductions establish up front the elements of an effective speech as outlined
here. They convey the theme in an interesting way. They make
a personal connection to the audience. They establish who you
are. And they draw the listeners in for more.

Organize your thoughts.

If you don't clearly know what you are trying to say, then you
can be sure that people who are new to the material and half

listening will definitely not know what you are trying to say. Make sure to pick a theme. Try to craft a catchy phrase for the theme that the audience can remember long after the speech. Repetition of the theme is critical. As to organization, most speech experts suggest dividing the speech into three parts: in the first part, tell them what you are going to tell them; in the second part, tell them; and in the third part, tell them what you just told them.

Connect to the audience.

An effective speech is not *given*; it is *received*. Therefore, it is critical to understand your audience. What are they interested in? What are their concerns? What is their experience level? Just as political speechwriters size up the anticipated audience of a speech, so should you. The personal touches about the group will make them think of you as one of them, and all people are more likely to respond positively to one of their own.

Be yourself.

You can excel as a public speaker only by being yourself. Use anecdotes from your own experiences to illustrate points. If you are thought of as funny, don't be afraid that well-placed humor will undercut the seriousness of your points. If you are a serious person, don't force humor. If you are casual, step away from the podium with a portable microphone. The audience can figure out if you are a phony or are uncomfortable.

Breathe.

Don't forget to stop for air. Good speeches have good pacing. Don't be afraid to slow down, to let your audience catch up and digest your point. Try silently counting to five between the major points of your speech.

Keep it brief.

Have you ever been disappointed in a speaker for being too brief with his or her remarks?! Not likely. Herman Herst Jr. captured the mind-set of most audiences with his remark "The easiest way to stay awake during an after-dinner speech is to deliver it." Don't give your audience a reason to snooze. Be short. Be sweet. Be brief.

How to Read the Newspaper Stock Tables

"The safest way to double your money is to fold it over and put it in your pocket."

—*Kin Hubbard*

As LONG AS you make money (or aspire to make money) you need a basic understanding of the financial world. One of the most critical tools of the financial world is the daily charts and tables that report the basic trading information of stocks and markets and appear in your daily newspaper. The most often-used tables are those listing the stocks on the NYSE, AMEX, and Nasdaq exchanges.

This chapter focuses on demystifying the seemingly endless sea of numbers that appear in stock tables. Don't worry, these tables only *appear* complex because of the volume of listings and the small type used. Most twelve-year-olds in investment clubs have no problem knowing what to look for, once they get the hang of it.

Remember, as they say in the investment business, past performance is no guarantee of future results. But, at least you now will know how to make stock history your guide.

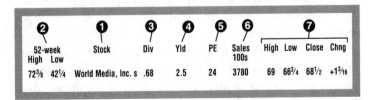

❷ 52-week High Low	❶ Stock	❸ Div	❹ Yld	❺ PE	❻ Sales 100s	❼ High	Low	Close	Chng
72⅜ 42¼	World Media, Inc. s	.68	2.5	24	3780	69	66¾	68½	+1³⁄₁₆

(1) Company names are listed alphabetically. Note that a company may have more than one outstanding issue of equity. A **pf** or **pr** symbol or a **w** symbol following the company name indicates that the listing is for preferred stock or a warrant, respectively. If the company had a recent stock split, an **s** will

appear. If the stock was newly issued in the past fifty-two weeks, an **n** will appear.

(2) The left-hand column gives the fifty-two-week trading range of the particular issue of equity. The greater the range in terms of percentage, the more volatile the stock.

Boldface quotations highlight stocks whose price changed by 5 percent or more in the previous trading day. <u>Underlined quotations</u> highlight the forty stocks on each exchange whose trading volume varied the most compared with their average-trading-day volume.

(3) The **Div** column refers to the cash dividend per share per year. Increasingly, many companies (particularly technology companies that invest earnings back into internal growth) pay no dividend, as indicated by an empty space in this column.

(4) **Yld**—yield percent—is the amount of cash dividends per share per year expressed as a percentage of the stock's trading price.

(5) The **PE** column presents the all-important price-earnings ratio. This ratio allows comparison of relative values of companies within industry segments. For example, shares of World Media are trading at 24 times their earnings. (Using PE ratios makes you sound very smart, so try to get this down enough to fake it.)

(6) The **Sales** column reports the trading volume in hundreds of shares.

(7) The last four columns mark the previous-trading-day range and close. Prices are listed in fractions of dollars; for example, ⅛ is 12½ cents, or .125.

Before you run off to invest with this new shred of knowledge, keep in mind that becoming a good investor of your personal finances requires study and practice. Of the thousands of books written over the last half century, the following four (four!) will teach you just about all you need to know: *The Intelligent Investor* by Benjamin Graham, *The Money Masters* by John Train, *One Up on Wall Street* by Peter Lynch, and *Buffet: The Making of an American Capitalist* by Roger Lowenstein.

Four Beginning Steps to Managing Your Money

Step 1: Get an account. Open a brokerage account with an account executive you trust or who comes recommended to you. If you will be choosing most of your own investments, a discount brokerage such as Charles Schwab & Co. works well.

Step 2: Learn the basics. Familiarize yourself with financial terminology, basic investment instruments, and market indicators. Do this by reading the four books recommended in this section, as well as regular editions of the *Wall Street Journal, Barron's, Money*, and *The Motley Fool* (www.motleyfool.com).

Step 3: Build a base. For the average beginner, invest about 25 percent of your savings in individual stocks and about 25 percent in stock mutual funds. Follow these investments for six months or so. Apply what you learn to investing the remainder of your money. For those under age thirty-five, invest 90 percent of your total disposable savings (money you will not need in the next six months) in equities—mutual funds and common stocks.

Step 4: Invest regularly. Each month, have 10 to 20 percent of your net pay automatically moved into your investment account. Do not try to predict market highs and lows, but rather invest in mutual funds and common stocks on a regular basis.

Lawyers—When You Need One and How to Choose One

> "I don't want a lawyer to tell me what I cannot do; I hire them to tell me how to do what I want to do."
>
> — *J.P. Morgan*

WHEN TROUBLE COMES around, you'd best be advised how to make a lawyer your ally. Even if trouble *never* comes around, you will likely need a lawyer a few times in your life. Buying or selling a house? Need a lawyer. Advice on small business affairs? Need a lawyer. Getting a divorce? Need a lawyer. Preparing a will? Need a lawyer.

Choosing a Lawyer

The best way to choose a lawyer is through referrals from friends or colleagues. Look for a lawyer who is experienced in the area in which you're consulting him. Set up an informational appointment for you to meet your prospective lawyer and discuss at a top level your situation and how he does business. You will be working closely with him and taking his counsel, so make sure he is your man. A man in legal need must feel as comfortable with his lawyer as a woman in labor feels with her obstetrician.

Paying a Lawyer

Your payment options are three: (1) flat fee, (2) contingency fee, and (3) hourly fee. A flat fee arrangement means you will pay your lawyer a fixed dollar amount no matter what—regardless of outcome or of time he puts in. Generally, this is not a good arrangement, as the attorney has no real incentive to prioritize your project. A contingency fee arrangement means that the lawyer will receive a percentage of what you recover in the case. This arrangement works well but is used only in personal injury cases in which you are seeking damages. An hourly fee arrangement is the most common. Your lawyer will let you know his billing rate up front (usually $125 to $300 per hour, depending on the experience of the lawyer, the type of law, and the region of the country) and the practice's policy on your also paying for expenses related to your case. It is a good idea to ask for an estimate of what the case will cost. Remember that in an hourly arrangement, his time *is* your money, so keep it focused and keep it all business.

Arresting Thoughts

The unthinkable has happened (the *very* unthinkable, to your babe and your employer!)—you have been arrested. (I know, I know, she was just helping you fix your brake pedal in that dark alley.) Whatever the charge—valid or not—circumstances demand that you think clearly and follow these rules:

1. Say nothing. Talk to nobody. Your only speaking part in this play is "My name is _____, and I want a lawyer."

2. Ask for your one constitutional phone call. Use this Monopoly card to get out of jail. Call someone who can pick you up at the police station and, if necessary, post bail for you. Most important, *call someone who is likely to be home.*

3. Hire a lawyer. Get the best you can afford. As the Miranda warning states, however, "If you cannot afford one, the court will appoint one for you." Who ever said you can't get something for nothing?

4. If you do run afoul of the law, the real world looks more like *NYPD Blue* than *Mayberry RFD*. Take it seriously; now that you are out of the jurisdiction of local juvenile court, your possible punishment is more than restitution and no TV for a month.

Part IV

Sports and Gaming

Golfing with the Boss

"If you break 100, watch your golf. If you break 80, watch your business."

—*Joey Adams*

"HEY, WE NEED a fourth tomorrow; do you want to join us at the links?" Mr. Bigboss barks. So begins the flameout of many meteoric careers. You are not just knocking the white pellet around with the fellows on a fun, sunny day—you are being observed and judged. You are golfing for success.

Golfing for success is how you play the game. Your boss will score you not on pars, but rather on how pleasant you were to play with and how you carried yourself during the round. Some famous golf sayings illuminate the basic truths of golf and the man.

1. *"Golf is a good walk spoiled."* (Mark Twain)
    Don't ever let your playing partners think you feel this way. Golfers are serious about enjoying their golf and scorn those who are not. Fanatic golfers think a good round of golf is better than money or sex. You are either with them or against them, and a true golfer will not bond with or respect a nongolfer. Your goal is to be good enough not to hurt the game of the other players in your foursome, and not too good to show them up. It's a delicate balance.

2. *"Drive for show, putt for dough."* (Bobby Locke)
    An incompetent golfer is an incompetent professional. How can they name you head of the new division when you keep topping drives? What kind of confidence is engendered by numerous yips? The drive is necessary for those in leadership positions. It is

about macho. It is about umph. The putt is necessary to be thought of as a winner. Clutch people make clutch putts. Those who make the sidehill four-footers when the press is on will deliver the sale, the presentation, the deal, every time.

3. *"A day spent in a round of strenuous idleness."*
   (William Wordsworth)
   Do not be blind to what is really going on during a five-hour round. It is anything but idle. Who gets to ride with the key client or boss? That person is closest to favor and power. How does the foursome pair up as the players walk down the fairway? Those relationships are deeper and will pay dividends. You will never have a better opportunity to form a bond on a personal level that will strengthen your professional relationship. That being said, be careful not to be too intrusive. A quiet golfer does not want to be bothered. Follow the lead established by your host/boss/client. Do they want to talk a lot? What do they like to talk about?

4. *"Give me my golf clubs, fresh air, and a beautiful woman, and you can keep my golf clubs and the fresh air."*
   (Jack Benny)
   What Jack Benny and most men know is that golf is a real male-bonding experience. (And the sport that gave rise to "golf widows.") From the putting green to the round to the showers to the postgame drink or card game, you and your fellow men will get closer. You need to be comfortable with the country-club, girl-talking, cigar-chomping, male hanging-out scene. Only a man's man can get to the top in the business world. Have manners, but be comfortable with those with none. Have a few well-chosen, brief jokes. Know and participate in the betting games, but don't be a shark.

5. *"If there is larceny in a man, golf will bring it out."*
   (Paul Gallicao)
   Golf displays the real character of a man. An
   improved lie in tough rough is the first step to
   inflated sales reports. A round of golf is filled with
   opportunities that show whether you are a stand-up
   guy or not. Count all your strokes. Be a bold, yet
   prudent shot-maker. There are no mulligans in life.

Golfing Goofs

More than any other sport, golf demands manners. *Caddyshack*
is a funny movie, but it is not full of role models. Do *not* do
any of the following:

1. Bring a date (it is not putt-putt).

2. Say, "Your swing doesn't look good today."

3. Walk over a putting line.

4. Whisper during a backswing.

5. Ask for a gimmee.

6. Wear matching Shark gear (did you think Geranimals
   were cool in grade school?).

7. Improve your lie.

8. Fail to repair a ball mark.

9. Complain that your new grips/new glove/new clubs
   are hurting your game.

10. Forget to pay off a golf bet immediately after the
    round.

Fishing 101

"In our family, there was no clear line between religion and fly fishing."

—A River Runs Through It
by Norman MacLean

"A fishing rod is a stick with a hook at one end and a fool at the other."

—*Samuel Johnson*

Is FISHING A pastime, a sport, or a higher calling? Never take the side that it is a pastime (at best) with a true fisherman unless you want to alienate him for life. For your purposes (getting in good with a real fisherman), remember that fishing is an extraordinary sport that demands hand-eye coordination, stamina, an artful touch, and great patience that never dulls a quick reflex.

Fishing began when man met water. The sport of fishing is almost as old, and its history, pace, and beauty make it a favorite of Fortune 500 executives, almost as much as golf. Before you cast into your boss's back or hook your best client on your line, get the Fishing 101 basics down.

Catching fish—and looking and acting like a pro while doing so—requires four things:

1. Fishing gear

2. Fish

3. An attempt to catch fish

4. Fishing protocol

Let's get you ready for your inaugural big day of fishing in ten minutes, OK?

Requirement #1: Fishing Gear

There are two basic groups of fishing gear: the gear you fish with, and the gear you wear.

Among rods, reels, lines, lures, flies, and other bait, there is just too much to know when it comes to the gear you fish with. It's not like buying a set of golf clubs, or even skis and boots, as the fishing gear required varies from outing to outing (due to factors such as the type of water in which you are fishing, the conditions of the day, and the type of fish you are looking to catch). Your solution? Borrow or rent. Either borrow from the "experts" you will be fishing with, or rent gear from your guide or the local tackle shop.

The gear you wear, however, is worth studying and purchasing. If you dress properly, a fishing day will never be a disaster, regardless of your fish input. When you are fishing, the cold feels colder, the sun seems brighter, and the wet never dries. Not only does the weather change from day to day and region to region, but it also changes from morning to afternoon. Flexibility—read *layers*—is the key.

If you don't already have the following items, visit an outdoor-gear store to get outfitted. Suit up in this order as you head out for a day of fishing:

- Underwear—Regular cotton T-shirt and bottoms.

- Long underwear—Both long-sleeved top and long bottoms. Go with a lightweight grade in silk or silk/cotton blend.

- Socks—Use the same socks that you would for skiing or hiking.

- Turtleneck—Helps protect your neck from wind.

- Pants—Flannel-lined are the best in cold weather. Any jeans or khaki will do, though.

- Fleece pullover—Use your ski liner or weekend football game Polartec.

- Rain jacket and pants—Gortex fabrics are the only ones that really repel wetness, and these fabrics are also the most breathable, keeping you from feeling as if you're trapped in a steam room. Although they are expensive (about $500 for pants and jacket), if you don't already have a Gortex rain suit, buy one. They also work great as golf rain gear.

- Waders—An absolute must if you will be angling from the water. You can either rent waders from a fishing-gear store or get them from your guide. The most effective style for keeping out water is the single-piece wader, consisting of boots, pants, and overalls. The best waders for any cold-water fishing are made of neoprene, the fabric used in diving wet suits.

- Fishing vest—They really are helpful in organizing your accessories (as well as being pretty cool-looking). Check them out at Orvis or L. L. Bean. Not a necessity if your inaugural fishing weekend will also be your last.

- Hat—A must. Your headgear must keep the sun out of your eyes and keep your head warm. You can accomplish these things with a baseball cap and a ski-type headband, or a ski hat and sunglasses, or if you are willing to go for it—the *flats hat*, the goofy-looking fishing hat with flip-down earflaps.

- Accessories—The six you should not leave home without: (1) sunscreen, (2) insect repellent, (3) small fishing first-aid kit, (4) granola or power bars, (5) Crokies-brand eyeglass securer, and (6) a waterproof disposable camera (just in case the big one comes in!).

Requirement #2: Fish

The saying "Fish where the fish are" is most telling in its literal context. You should aim to fish in waters that have enough fish for a beginner. And the most enjoyable fishing combines great natural beauty with fish o' plenty. The world is filled with jaw-dropping fishing spots, some of the most famous including bone fishing on Christmas Island, just north of the equator off Honolulu; marlin on Great Barrier Reef, Australia; rainbow trout in Bristol Bay, Alaska; and largemouth bass in the fresh-water Everglades, Florida. True fishermen will chew your ear off with stories of perfect and plentiful little mountain streams. The point of all this? Once you leave your local pond, you don't need to worry that much about this requirement.

Requirement #3: An Attempt to Catch Fish

The goal of a beginner is to catch a fish. The goal of an inter-mediate fisherman is to catch a lot of fish. The goal of an advanced fisherman is to catch big fish. The goal of an expert is to catch a lot of big fish. In each stage of a fisherman's sport-ing life, three words sum up the best way to accomplish the goal: *get a guide.*

For beginners, a fishing guide provides the comfort of doing everything other than holding the rod. Guides will take the lead in selecting the best spots to fish, choosing and set-ting bait, counseling on setting the hook and casting, and, if you are fortunate, photographing you with your catch and then setting it free. For all levels of anglers, a guide can help teach the nuances of the local waters, enhancing the experience. The best source of good guides is references. But before you book any guide, talk to him on the phone to make sure he understands your desires for the outing.

Keep these words of background in mind regarding the bait, rods, line, and casting used in the attempt to catch fish, so you know what the guide is doing for you and can participate more intelligently in the attempt. Fish is caught with bait, and choosing the type of bait is an art, with the goal to determine what the fish may be looking to eat. Most anglers use lures—artificial bait—as they are easier, provide more flexibility, and can be reused after nibbles, thus allowing more time for fishing. There are three basic types of rods—bait-casting, spinning, and fly-fighting—with most made of a graphite/fiberglass composite. Rods tend to be classified by their bendability (or action) and weight. The line type and weight varies with the equipment being used and the fish being sought. Casting, especially fly casting, is one of the great pleasures when mastered and one of the great embarrassments when not. So, spend some time studying the fundamentals beforehand, and do not be shy about asking for help from your guide.

Requirement #4: Fishing Protocol

- Your goal as a beginner on a fishing outing is to stay out of the way and not impede the enjoyment of your fellow fishermen. This includes not sulking if you are shut out.

- Don't talk. And never, ever talk business. Fishing is not for the chatty.

- Do take along fine cigars and fine wine. Your comrades will remember you as a good provider, not a bad fisherman.

- Do ask your guide for help. And let him help you get your allotment when the day runs long.

- Don't take a pager, cell phone, or radio. People fish to get away from it all and take in the natural beauty.

- Remember that the worst day fishing beats the best day in the office. OK, you may not think so, but real fisherman do, so play along.

Waxing the K2s

"You simply let yourself go, gliding delightfully over the gentle slopes, flying down the steeper ones, taking an occasional cropper, but getting as near to flying as any earth-bound man can."

—*Sir Arthur Conan Doyle*

SKIING, MORE THAN any other sporting activity, provides an intense relationship to nature. Crisp, clean air. Dazzling sparkle of the sun off the snow. Brilliant colors and grandeur of high mountain scenery. Take it all in as you ascend the mountain. Attack it, *live* it as you plunge back down.

But since you are more likely to live in Chicago than Sun Valley, your number of skiing days is limited, as is the opportunity to pick up the critical skill of waxing your skis. The properly waxed ski is a performing, longer-living, and happy ski. Treat your skis right and they will treat you right.

Step 1. **Buy some wax.** Any real ski shop, and most good general sporting-goods stores, will carry ski wax. There are many kinds. The biggest difference among them is the outdoor temperature to which the wax is best tailored. Since the weather, like much else in skiing, is unpredictable, select a wax recommended for the coldest temperature you expect over your ski outing. The correct wax for the outdoor conditions will provide the optimal hardness on the bottom of the ski meeting the snow. Coated with the ideal hardness, the ski bottom will propel you effortlessly, especially over flat areas which otherwise require poling and generally unpleasant effort.

Step 2. **File ski edges.** Even with great snow conditions, rocks and twigs take a toll on metal ski edges. Ski edges need to be sharp and smooth to aid the ski in turning and holding firmly on steeper slopes. Feel the edges with your fingers. Take a file (purchase a special one from a ski shop or use a light-grade nail file or sandpaper) to any rough spots, first running the file flat across the surface and then at a right angle to the ski. Work the rough spots until the ski edge is burr free and reasonably sharp.

Step 3. **Apply the wax.** Rub the wax over the bottom of the ski, preferably using a cotton rag (paper towels or fingers also work). Apply the wax in a thin, even coat, making sure that no areas are uncovered. You can see where the wax is as it appears like a dull film. The top six to twelve inches or so at the tip where the ski curls do not need waxing.

Step 4. **Heat the wax.** The big final step. Heating the wax allows it to seep into the fine crevices and solidify to the ski bottom. The best way to heat the wax is with an old iron. Using a medium setting, run the heated iron over the waxed ski in a long, smooth motion similar to painting. If you don't have an iron, use a hair dryer to generate the heat necessary to melt the wax, and then spread the wax with your fingers. It is more difficult to get an even coat with this method.

Waxing your K2s (or other brand of skis) should take about ten minutes. The waxing will last two to four ski days. Last one to the bottom of the run buys the first round!

The Twenty-Minute No-Equipment Workout

> " 'How long does getting thin take?'
> Pooh asked anxiously."
>
> —Winnie the Pooh
> *by A. A. Milne*

WORKING OUT IS boring. Working out is painful. Unfortunately, working out is necessary—necessary to look good, and necessary to stay healthy. The biggest hurdles to overcome are (1) breaking out of your couch's gravity pull to get to the health club and (2) finding enough time among earning your first million, discovering your dream girl, and sleeping eight hours a night to do it. The following twenty-minute no-equipment workout removes these obstacles—all you need under this plan is yourself and some discipline.

Exercise #1: The Warm-Up/Flexibility

Unless you want your quadriceps snapping faster than a nun's ruler, the warm-up is critical. Even Michael Jordan and Emmitt Smith do it before they lace their signature sneakers.

Toe Touch

Stand straight and bend down from the waist toward your toes. Slowly come closer to touching the top of your feet. Bend your knees slightly and push until you're *slightly* uncomfortable. (Be very careful if you have back problems.) Repeat ten times.

Arm Circle

Stand straight with arms out to the side, parallel to the floor. Move your arms alternatively clockwise and counterclockwise in increasingly larger circles. Perform one minute.

Thigh Stretch

Sit on the floor with your legs forming a diamond pattern (put the soles of your feet together). Gently push your knees toward the floor while the soles stay together. Perform one minute.

Knee Pull

Lie on your back. Flex one knee while the other remains extended. Grasp the flexed knee with your hands and pull it toward your chest. Hold the position for thirty seconds. Repeat three times.

Exercise #2: Push-Ups/Upper Body

Any exercise that's embraced by both marines *and* prisoners is worth considering. I know you'll feel as if you're in fifth-grade gym again, but properly done, push-ups can strengthen and tone your chest, shoulders, triceps, and fingers all in one simple exercise.

Place your hands on the floor at shoulder width. Keep your legs straight behind you and your chin up. Do not arch your back. Lower your chest so that it just touches the floor. Each repetition should be deliberate, just as you would handle the bench press. Start trying to do one set of ten perfect push-ups in a minute. Your goal is three sets of twenty—each set in a minute with a minute rest in between. I said it's a *goal*.

The beauty of the push-up is the ability to work different muscles by slightly changing your form. To work your chest more, widen your hand and arm position. To emphasize your shoulders, execute the reps with your feet up on a chair (very tough!). For finger and wrist strength, try the push-ups on your fingertips.

Exercise #3: Sit-Ups/Abs and Back

A tried-and-true favorite. Make sure you are on carpet or a workout mat. Lie on the floor with your feet together and knees bent up about a foot off the floor. Place your hands in fists on either side of your head. Using your stomach muscles, slowly pull yourself up until your chin hits your knees. Slowly pull back down. Focus. Maintain control and tension at all times. Do not "rock" yourself up and back as you did the last time you did sit-ups. Start with one set of fifteen per minute at a minimum. Your goal is three sets of thirty—each set in a minute with a minute of rest in between.

Exercise #4: Jogging/Cardiofitness

The last muscle to strengthen and tone is your heart. A good jog will provide an overall body workout inside and out. A Nordictrack, treadmill, or Stairmaster will provide a great cardiofitness workout if you have already sprung for one of those dust-collecting modern sculptures. Target a two-mile run (or machine-equivalent workout) with an increasingly faster time. After three months, you should be able to do a ten-minute mile.

Before you decide to blow off this simple regimen, consider the many ancillary benefits of staying fit beyond your actual health. Sticking with the program will tend to make you more confident and more aggressive. Women will respond to this attitude even before you have added an inch to your chest. Soon you will actually look better, magnifying your appeal. Over time you will be trimmer, allowing your favorite Armani to fit again. And you will also feel and be better, adding ten years to your wonderful life.

The Poker Primer

"If you sit down at the poker table and you
can't tell who the sucker is, you are it."

—*Old gambling saying*

AFTER THE COMPANY Christmas dinner, you're invited into the
annual poker game with the firm's other fast-rising executives.
Although it is estimated that 20 million people play poker, you
do not. *Holdem, Lowball, Stud, Night Baseball, High-Low, Draw
Trips to Win* . . . might as well be Nintendo games to you.

Poker, played in the United States since the early 1800s, is
an easy game to learn but a hard game to master. It is a game in
which each player controls much of his own fate. Many make
the mistake of considering poker a gambling game because it is
played for money. Luck plays a significant role in any given
evening, but over time, mathematically, the cards will even up
for all players. Thus, if you lose regularly, you are being outplayed.

To be a winning poker player you have to be versed in
money management, mathematical odds, and bluffing. Suggested reading includes *The Education of a Poker Player* by Herbert O. Yardley, *The Complete Guide to Winning Poker* by Albert
H. Morehead, *How to Make Over $1,000,000 Playing Poker* by
Doyle Brunson, and *Big Deal: A Year as a Professional Poker
Player* by Anthony Holden.

Here we deal only with the rules of the games to get you
started. Although there are literally hundreds of variations on
the game, they can generally be divided into three basic categories: draw, stud, and common card poker.

Draw Poker

In draw poker each player is dealt five cards face down. The
betting starts with the player to the left of the dealer. He may

either bet (except in some cases where the dealer has called that a pair of jacks is required to open) or check. As soon as the first round of betting is concluded, each player calling the opening bet, beginning with the person who opened, discards face down up to three cards and is dealt replacements. There is then a second round of betting, and the player with the highest hand who called the bets is the winner.

The absence of the information given by face-up cards in draw poker diminishes the advantages of more skilled opponents. If you don't know how to play poker well, draw poker is the game for you.

Stud Poker

The most common forms of stud poker deal each player five or seven cards. In five-card stud the sequence (unless otherwise specified by the dealer in advance) is ante, one card down and one card up, bet, one card up, bet, one card up, bet, one card up, bet. More people prefer seven-card stud because they feel that having more cards gives them a better chance at winning (when really it just increases the exposure of the novice with the additional betting round). In seven-card stud the standard sequence is ante, two cards down and one card up, bet, one card up, bet, one card up, bet, one card up, bet, one card down, bet. In each game, a player's hand is the best five-card hand.

Common Card Poker

Common card games take numerous forms, with the key feature being that certain cards will be shared by the players remaining in the game. The game played in the $1,000,000 World Series of Poker in Las Vegas is a common card game called Texas Holdem. In Texas Holdem each player is dealt two cards face down. After a round of betting, three cards are turned up all at once in the center of the table (the flop) which are the property of all the players. The sequence then continues with bet, one common card up, bet, one common card up, bet. The player may select any five of the seven cards (two of the player's own, five that are common) to make the best hand.

So, What Beats What, Again?

From highest to lowest the following is the rank of poker hands:

Royal flush—10-J-Q-K-A of the same suit

Straight flush—five cards in sequence in the same suit, such as 5-6-7-8-9 of spades

Four of a Kind—such as four kings

Full house—three of a kind and one pair

Flush—five cards in the same suit that are not in sequence

Straight—five cards in sequence that are not in the same suit

Three of a Kind—such as three 9s

Two pairs—such as K-K-8-8 (The other card can be used to break ties.)

One pair—such as Q-Q (The other cards can be used to break ties.)

Poker, as all sporting pursuits, demands training. Try to attain as much experience as cheaply as possible. Play in groups at your skill level. Watch the hands you drop out of. Deal practice hands to yourself at your dining room table and study the flow of the cards. Take imaginary positions—at each critical point try to predict the two strongest hands—then study how they turn out. Always do a postmortem of each poker session. What was luck? What was a good bluff? What was a good bet?

Leave a chair open for me. Players wild and the sky's the limit.

Part V

Etiquette

Manners and the Man

"Manners make the fortune of
the ambitious youth."

—*Ralph Waldo Emerson*

MANNERS ARE NOW more important than ever. As the world
becomes a more barbaric place, the exercise of subtle, everyday
courtesies can distinguish you to friends, family, dates, and colleagues. So few human beings have manners these days that the
use of them now automatically connotes intelligence, breeding,
style, and sophistication, even when none of those qualities
exist.

Following are "twenty-five by twenty-five"—twenty-five
manners that should be part of your habits by the time you are
age twenty-five. Stick a copy of this page in your wallet and
carry it with you until you've got the basics down.

1. **Gossip.** Go ahead and listen; but don't pass it on.
   Better to garner a reputation as a man who can be
   trusted with delicate information. This will engender
   confidence in you *and* ensure that you keep hearing
   the office butt.

2. **Eye Contact.** Look people in the eye—it inspires
   trust. It also assures women that you are not staring at
   their breasts.

3. **Physical Contact.** No hands on shoulders, touches on
   the arm, or pats on the back to anyone with whom
   you are not in a dating relationship or football huddle.

4. **Sex.** Do unto others . . .

5. **Sex Again.** Don't kiss and tell (OK, you are allowed
   the best-friend rule).

6. **One-Night Stands.** Use a condom. And give it your best effort.

7. **Public Affection.** Manners meets passion in a battle royal. As they say in Vegas, pick 'em.

8. **Drinking.** Never to excess in a business setting. Never drink and drive.

9. **Smoking.** Smoking as a habit is gross, rude, and unhealthy and should be broken.

10. **Chewing Gum.** Reserved for hookers, baseball players, and wise guys.

11. **Gambling.** OK to do. Not OK not to pay up. Settle your debts immediately, even if you have to float a bad check for a few days.

12. **Guests.** Treat them as such, making sure they are comfortable, have what they want, and enjoy themselves. Think of yourself as a hotel or restaurant proprietor.

13. **Overnight Guests.** Your uncle was right: guests, like fish, stink after forty-eight hours. Don't wear out your welcome.

14. **Uninvited Guests.** Don't be one or bring one—they are uninvited for a reason.

15. **Guest Gifts.** As a party guest, take a small offering (such as a bottle of wine or a nice bunch of flowers). As an overnight guest, send a note and a gift (such as a plant) after your visit.

16. **Pets.** As a host, be sensitive to the allergies of your guests, and always keep Fido from licking and leg humping. I know it's hard for pet owners/lovers to understand, but pets are not people.

17. **Kids.** Unless they are specifically invited, they are always uninvited guests. And if you are with people who don't have kids, don't talk for more than three minutes, tops, about yours.

18. **Thank-You Notes.** So critical for all who want to get ahead that they have their own chapter in this book (see page 106).

19. **Gifts.** Try not to let an important occasion go unnoticed. For friends and family, at least send a card with a short note, even if you are not in the habit of exchanging gifts.

20. **Conversations.** Don't dominate conversations, and don't interrupt.

21. **Correcting People.** Never in public, even when you know they're wrong—unless it is personally about you, your woman, or your mom.

22. **Receiving Compliments.** Being the stud that you are, you'll find the compliments will come. Simply respond "Thank you"—graciously.

23. **Jokes.** Use rarely among business colleagues, and never tell off-color jokes.

24. **Response to Jokes.** Obviously, laugh if the joke is funny. But if a colleague or friend tells offensive stories or off-color jokes, you should discuss your feelings about the appropriateness of it in private. Do not reprimand him in a crowd, and do not just let it go.

25. **Timeliness.** Be on time. This is the cardinal, and most often broken, rule of manners. The rule does not apply in Los Angeles and New York City.

Manners and the Man—Part 2

"Etiquette is today what it has always been: a code of behavior based on kindness, consideration and unselfishness—something that should not, and will not, ever change. But manners, derived as they are from etiquette, must change to keep up with the ever-changing world in which we live."

—*Emily Post*

ELIZABETH POST, the granddaughter-in-law of the legendary Emily Post, recently published the 15th edition of Emily Post's *Etiquette*, a 783-page tome of rules, regulations, and guidelines as to the rights and wrongs of social interaction. It appears that manners may be even more important for the success of the modern man than one may think.

So, another "twenty-five by twenty-five" is in order. Really.

1. **Elevators and Doors.** Hold them open for elderly people and women, and when feasible, for men and kids as well. But be practical in cramped situations.

2. **Gentlemanly Touches.** It's the little things that certain kinds of women love: carrying her bag, holding an umbrella over her head in the rain, helping her off and on with her coat.

3. **To Rise or Not to Rise.** Generally, stand when your date or a woman in your party stands to leave or approaches to sit. This is also a good rule for top bosses and other business dignitaries.

4. **Remarks.** Many guys think they are endearing themselves by making what they believe is a clever remark to a woman about her new outfit or haircut. Understand that most women find all remarks about them that are not clearly a compliment, *definitively not funny.*

5. **The Check.** In date contexts, the inviter is expected to be the payer. Friends or couples should pay for their own meals and entertainment. Note, this is not always the same as "splitting" the check, in that each person or couple may have very different orders (such as one couple not drinking any of the bottle of wine).

6. **Keeping Plans.** You have no obligation to accept an invitation. But once you do accept, you must attend.

7. **Guest for a Meal.** It is OK to pass on any item, provided it is not the main dish.

8. **At the Table.** The big three: Chew with your mouth closed. Keep your elbows off the table. Don't reach.

9. **Away from the Table.** Sneeze, cough, blow your nose, pick your teeth, comb your hair, and use other personal items away from the table. People never forgive a gross-out guest.

10. **Utensils.** Always start with the utensil farthest from the plate. Don't ask why. Just do it.

11. **The Napkin.** Place it on your lap as soon as your date or hostess does the same. Do not tuck it in your collar—better to spill on one good tie than look like a goof 100 times over.

12. **Tipping.** Know the rules to get ahead—see "Proper Tipping—When, Who, and How Much," page 110.

13. **Office Casual.** Putting up your feet on the desk, taking off your shoes, or rolling up your sleeves is never acceptable—even if your boss does it.

14. **Office Talk.** Generally best kept to a minimum. Keep it friendly, but all business. Do not inquire about others' personal matters beyond "How was your weekend?"

15. **Prejudice.** Is not cool. Rise above it—you will look good and feel better.

16. **Honesty.** Although it's hokey, it really is the best policy.

17. **Negativity.** Is bad. Be positive. If you can't be honest and positive, politely demur.

18. **Telephone—Outgoing Calls.** Do not call someone at home before 9 A.M. or after 9 P.M. Always identify yourself when calling.

19. **Telephone—Incoming Calls.** If you receive a message on your answering machine, you must return the call at an appropriate time, but always within two days. There is no obligation to have an answering machine or to answer the phone.

20. **Telephone—General.** Do not eat, type on your computer, or listen to TV in the background when you're on the phone. Use call waiting only as necessary to take down a phone number.

21. **Introductions I.** Always use full names in introductions. Introduce women first.

22. **Introductions II.** If you do not know the name of a person you are put in the position of introducing, then introduce the person you know to the other and hope that person in turn introduces him- or herself. If this fails, graciously admit your memory lapse and move on.

23. **Introductions III.** The key is to remember names. The main memory trick to this is to repeat the name once it is introduced to you—"Nice to meet you, Donn (or Mr. Davis)." If you heard the name wrong, or not at all, this is your easy chance to get it right.

24. **Introductions IV.** People with titles ("Dr.," "Judge," "General," etc.) love them and resent those who do not use them in introductions. Also, if you're introducing a person who does not have a formal title but is nonetheless important (even if only in his or her own mind), let it be known—"This is Donn Davis, my boss and a famous author."

25. **Be Silently Smug.** Don't tell others they are rude or have exhibited bad manners. Just suck it up, smile, and revel in your manfully tasteful superiority.

The Only Thank-You Notes You'll Ever Need

"On certain occasions, a letter is the
only way to show that you are sincere,
which is sometimes necessary whether
you are or not."

—*Miss Manners*

LIKE GOOD TASTE, thank-you notes never go out of style. Don't
let others' failure to observe this indispensable display of gra-
ciousness lead you to make the same mistake. Timely and well-
written thank-you notes are among the bulwarks of a courteous,
civil society under constant siege from etiquette philistines.
They are also a genuine way to express gratitude and appreciation and demonstrate your own class in the process.

The most important features of a thank-you note have
nothing to do with what they say. What really counts is this:
you must be prompt; you generally must handwrite the note;
and it must be on good, preferably personalized stationery. Like
most of life, style and showing up are 99 percent of the battle.

For most events promptness means within a week (a few
days is even better), although the time is extended for singu-
lar events where you've received a multitude of gifts, such as a
wedding or graduation. Don't despair, however, if you are late;
there are no deadlines for good manners, and a thank-you is
always better late than never.

The note should be handwritten when you want it to have
a personal feel. Typed or E-mail (if the person is technologi-
cally savvy) responses are most appropriate for business thank-
you notes, particularly in the context of interviews or other
situations in which you just met the person.

As to writing paper (the cool term for stationery), remember that your personality is displayed with every piece sent.

Don't overdue it with fancy papers, borders, colors, engravings, and symbols—your *writing* should express your flair. Buy a nice monarch-size sheet (about seven by ten inches) in cream or white with your name or initials engraved at the top in black, dark gray, hunter green, or navy. Have your return address engraved on the back flap of the envelope, and have the envelope lined in the same color as the printing. Keep it simple.

As for the contents of the thank-you note, use the three forms that follow as your guide, filling in the blanks as appropriate. Personalize and embellish as time and desire allow. After you've shot off a few of them with minimal effort and maximum appreciation from the recipients (not to mention from your mother, who somehow always finds out about these things), send me a thank-you note for this chapter!

Gift Thank-You (for birthdays, Christmas, graduation, etc.)

Dear _____,

Thank you so much for the _____. It was very generous and thoughtful. I especially like the [color, style, etc.] [It will prove particularly useful because _____.] or [I had been wanting a _____ because _____.] I really appreciate your thinking of me.

[Thanks again] [Love],

_____

Hospitality Thank-You
(for dinners, parties, outings, etc.)

Dear _____,

Thank you so much for having me [to dinner] [at your party] [to play golf] on [insert date]. I really enjoyed seeing your [beautiful home] [great country club], and the [food was delicious] [golf game (other than mine) was terrific]. I also appreciated the opportunity to spend some time with you [and _____] [and to meet _____].

Thanks again for a wonderful _____,

Sincerely,

_____

Business Thank-You (for interviews, meeting, etc.)

Dear _____ :

Thank you for taking the time to [meet] [talk] with me on [insert date]. I really appreciated the opportunity to [learn about] [discuss] _____ .

[I am confident that I would serve [company name] well as [job title] and that I would truly enjoy the position.] [I believe we share similar business philosophies and would be able to [establish a] [enhance the existing] value-creating relationship.]

[Insert sentence regarding appropriate planned follow-up.]

Sincerely,

_____

Proper Tipping—When, Who, and How Much

"I don't believe in tipping."
"That's un-American."

—*Dialogue from the film*
Reservoir Dogs, *written
and directed by Quentin
Tarantino*

TIPPING IS THE grease of the capitalistic engine. Without a tipping system that is understood and followed by most consumers, service industries as we know them would deteriorate. Cappuccino would increasingly be delivered slow and cold. Taxis would blare unintelligible rap music while careening from lane to lane. And, the cable guy would show up late—well, some things are beyond hope.

Vary your tips according to service received to keep entrepreneurial hustle alive. Your tipping tips, sir:

Travel Tipping Guide

Taxi/Private Car: 20 percent of fare (deduct 5 percent each for squawking CB radio, driver smoking without permission, no air-conditioning, or unsafe driving).

Sky Caps: $1 per bag checked.

Doorman, Bellman: $1 for calling a cab; $1 per bag handled.

Delivery to Hotel Room (fax, etc.): $2.

Room Service: 25 percent (*including* the preassessed charges).

Concierge: $3 per task; $10 per major task (such as obtaining tickets to a sold-out show).

Restaurant Tipping Guide

Waiter: 20 percent (minimum $1 per person per table).

Bartender, Wine Steward: 15 percent of alcohol bill.

Buffet Staff: 10 percent.

Maître d': Not necessary (unless a table or other special treatment was requested and received).

Busboy: Not necessary.

Coat Valet: $1 per item.

Car Valet: $2 to $5, depending on proximity, weather, and model of car.

Personal Services Tipping Guide

Haircut: 15 to 20 percent.

Massage and Spa Services: 20 percent.

Topless Dancer: What you see is what you give.

Home Delivery (groceries, pizza, florist): Depending on weather and size of order—$3 to $5.

Dry Cleaner: Necessary only for extraordinary help, such as emergency tux pressing or returning the cuff links left in your shirt—$3 to $5.

Phone Installation/Repair: No tip necessary—a God-given right.

Cable Installation: If you were to bill them for cleaning the mud off your carpet and the half vacation day you had to take waiting, *they* would owe you.

Year-End Tipping Guide

Letter Carrier: $20 (probably not deserved, but you must ensure that your mail keeps coming).

Newspaper Delivery: Ever wondered why they leave you that holiday card? Yep, include an extra $10 in your December payment.

Garbage Pickup, Lawn Care Service: $25 to $40 (to the driver, who is generally the crew manager, in an envelope, making sure to note your name and address).

Apartment/Condo Workers (doormen, maintenance staff): $50 to $150 in one lump sum with the management office (depending on size of the staff, expert nature of the service, and degree to which you rely on personal attention).

Maid, Nanny: One week's pay plus Christmas week off with pay.

All these hard-working service providers rely on tips to live. So, when they do their part, do your part.

How to Make a Toast

". . . men of few words are the best men . . ."
—*Shakespeare*

IT MAY BE the reception of a wedding in which you just stood up for the groom. It may be the engagement party or rehearsal dinner for your sister or brother. It may be an important birthday celebration for a family member or close friend. Or, it may be a going-away party for a close colleague at work. In each case, it is your time to stand up to deliver the big toast. Toasts, like speeches, can be a disaster if not handled as skillfully as a modern man should. Lift your glass and join me in these toasting tips.

Toasting Tip #1: You'll know if you should make a toast.

Only a few toasts at any function are called for (and can be tolerated). It is not rude to let the occasion go by without a toast from you if enough toasts have been given and you are not one of those closest to the honoree. Generally, it will either be obvious that a toast from you is a must, or you will have been requested in advance by the host or the honoree to prepare remarks.

Toasting Tip #2: Prepare and practice.

The two Ps help ensure that your toast will be the best it can be. Ask others to give you an evaluation of the appropriateness of the content. As with any public speaking occasion, both what you say and how you say it will be remembered.

Toasting Tip #3: Deliver it from the heart.

Mean what you say and say what you mean. Sincerity shows through and makes up for most other shortcomings of toasts. Concentrate on the core, unique qualities that you admire in or enjoy about the honoree.

Toasting Tip #4: Be careful of humor.

Light humor can be effective if done tastefully and with regard to the audience. Do *not* cross the fine line between humor and embarrassment. Stay away from the subjects of old girlfriends, sex, drinking, irresponsibility, and run-ins with the law. In professional settings, be careful recounting stories about busted deals, interoffice politics, work gripes of old, or money matters. And if you aren't funny, don't try to be.

Toasting Tip #5: Keep it brief.

Nobody finds fault with a short toast. Too many people feel that quantity of speech is necessary to show they really care about the honored guests. And, ironically, the longer the toast, the more you, rather than the subject of your toast, will be in the spotlight—a true *faux pas*. All will appreciate your keeping the toast to about one minute (even less if several toasts are expected).

Toasting Tip #6: Reply to the toasts.

If you are the person being toasted, try to take it all in stride if those toasting you have not read and followed this chapter. At the conclusion of all the toasts, stand and raise your glass in response. A simple "Thank you," or a brief toast in return, is appropriate.

Part VI

Looking Good

Suit Yourself

"Never underestimate the power
of what you wear."

—*Oscar E. Schoeffler,*
former editor of Esquire
magazine

TODAY CORPORATIONS ARE so big and the business environment
so fast-paced that higher-ups can't possibly keep daily tabs on
how great your work is. They do, however, notice whether you
look the part. The modern man who takes seriously the phrase
"It's not who you are, it's what you wear" has a Zegna up on
dressing for success.

Suit Step 1: Don't skimp.

If you are like the rest of us trying to make it big, sixty-hour
weeks are the norm. So, why skimp on the items you'll almost
literally spend your life in? Generally, the more expensive the
garment, the better the fabric, and top-quality wool fabrics will
look, wear, and feel better during twelve-hour-a-day battles. A
good rule of thumb is to spend as much on each suit as you
did on your main TV, or about half as much as you spent on
your complete stereo system, whichever is greater. Unlike your
entertainment hardware, your suits should pay for themselves
over and over again in raises and bonuses.

Suit Step 2: Just the basics, ma'am.

The work world is not about high fashion; it's about good, solid
dressing. So, go with the basics in your suits and shirts. Think
of your suit and shirt as the blank canvas, and your tie and

other details as the paint, the expression of your uniqueness (see Step 7). In suits, the best fabric is year-round-weight 100 percent worsted wool. Not wool crepe. Not flannel. Not some funky Italian weave.

The complete suit wardrobe can be accomplished with four suits: one solid dark gray, one gray pinstripe, one solid dark navy, and one navy pinstripe. In shirts, go white. It is impossible not to impress with 100 percent cotton broadcloth, straight-collar white shirts. Button-down collars (like your dad used to buy at Brooks Brothers) just do not cut the same formal, dashing image.

Suit Step 3: Dress to impress your boss, not your wife or girlfriend.

Woman want men to dress stylishly. They will be eager to apply the newest *Vogue* and *GQ* fashion trends to your wardrobe. Taking their advice may draw oohs from your girlfriend, your female colleagues, and women at happy hour, but it will not position you as the man to be reckoned with at work. Your boss is not going to know that this season's trendy color is ochre and that Versace sharkskin suits are all the rage in Milan. All your boss will know is that he doesn't like it.

Suit Step 4: Mimicry will take you far.

What suits are your boss (and your boss's boss) wearing? That, my friend, is what you should be wearing as well. Natural selection is alive and thriving in business—those in power tend to promote those who remind them of themselves, and that certainly includes their personal style. So, dress for the position you are targeting to demonstrate that you understand what the job entails.

Suit Step 5: It's all in the fit.

The bad news is that the suit won't be spending the day on its hanger or on that perfectly proportioned mannequin. It will be on you. The good news is that a properly fitted suit can truly hide an unfit body.

If your suit doesn't fit you in a flattering manner, you've lost the battle. When selecting a suit, make sure that the shoulders do not extend beyond your natural shoulders (David Byrne you are not) and that the chest fits—these areas can not be properly altered to fit you. Take the suit for a test walk around the store. Make sure it moves with you. Sit down—after all, this is how you'll spend most of your time in the suit—and make sure the pants are roomy enough in the hips and thighs.

As for tailoring your suit jacket, you want one-half inch of shirt showing at the cuff and three-fourths inch showing at the back collar. The pants should end at the top of your shoe heel in back, breaking on the top of your shoes in front. Have your suit pants tailored with either a 1½-inch or a 1¾-inch cuff.

Suit Step 6: Know thy salesperson.

Rarely likable, never trustworthy: that's a suit salesman. These guys work on commission, so they're likely to push you to buy, even if they don't have a suit that's quite right for you. Salesmen generally don't have a clue about the corporate office world, so they usually recommend "interesting" high fashion over "boring" business basics. All that said, it is smart to develop a relationship with one salesperson in order to get advanced word on sales, speedy tailoring, and preferential treatment if a return visit is necessary.

Suit Step 7: It's in the details.

The details separate the real dresser from the wanna-be. The most obvious sign of power, style, creativity—or lack thereof—in a man's work outfit is his tie. You *are* your tie, so choose carefully. Your best bet is to tie up from the four classic groups: power (exemplified by Hermes ties); business whimsical (signified by Ferragamo ties); classic (think Polo); and stylish solids (the Cary Grant look).

To express some personal style in suits, purchase one of your four basics in a three-button model or in a six-button double-breasted style. To express personal style in shirts, consider a French cuff, a pocketless front, or a small gray monogram on the left breast of the shirt. When you're feeling dashing, fold a white linen handkerchief into your suit chest pocket. Above all else, keep your socks pulled high and a shine on your shoes.

Your Friday (or Everyday) Casual Wardrobe

"The only thing that separates man from beast is the ability to accessorize."

—*Isaac Mizrahi*

MOST OF THE corporate world is unlikely to go casual all the time, since the decision makers have only suits to wear, but it's an inescapable fact that Casual Friday has swept the working world.

Casual Friday does *not* mean you dress as you would on Saturday, just one day earlier. Rather, there are basic sartorial standards for the new, informal workplace. Luckily, these standards have a few things in common. The clothes are cut more generously than traditional work clothes and thus are more comfortable and forgiving of body shape. The clothes are of natural fibers of wool, cotton, and linen, making them drape nicely and breathe easy. And, these standards tend to emphasize basics, allowing you to form the foundation of your casual wardrobe time efficiently and cost effectively.

A proper casual wardrobe needs to be simultaneously classic and fashionable. You must not appear either too trendy or too much of an undistinguished gentleman. The well-chosen wardrobe should last several years, with a few pieces being those you could grow old in. Once you get the following basics of your closet, you will always have something to wear on casual days.

Sport Coats

You can dress up (gray flannel slacks, a dress shirt and tie, even a contrasting vest) or down (jeans, a polo shirt, and sneakers) using a sport coat at the center. It is the most important weapon in your casual arsenal.

- 1 100 percent worsted-wool navy blazer—It should be single-breasted and medium all-seasons weight. Spend as much money as you can here, as you will probably wear it fifty times a year. If the jacket does not already sport gold or silver buttons, you should add them (from a local button store or from a catalog such as Ben Silver).

- 1 additional sport coat for the spring/summer seasons—Choose a 100 percent linen blazer in black or navy. Preferably, a three-button, more unconstructed style. Great for all occasions—particularly when going out.

- 1 additional sport coat for the fall/winter seasons—Choose a camel-hair or black-and-white houndstooth blazer. Both fabrics work great with a variety of trousers and shirts. Also, both dress up and down almost as well as the stalwart navy blazer.

Trousers

Keep your jeans and wrinkled Gap khakis for the weekend. For the casual workweek acquire the following seven basic trousers. Most can be purchased from a fine store such as Neiman-Marcus or Saks Fifth Avenue or from your local Banana Republic or Brooks Brothers. They can also be found in the Polo sections of your local department store or ordered from the J Crew catalog.

- 2 pairs dress khakis (100 percent cotton).

- 1 pair medium gray trousers (flannel if you live in the colder East or Midwest).

- 1 pair brown twill dress trousers (cotton or wool).

- 1 pair navy trousers (100 percent worsted wool, preferably a fuller Italian cut).

- 1 pair wide-wale corduroys in black or olive.

- 1 pair linen trousers in tan or olive.

Sport Shirts/Sweaters/Vests

It is here that you should let more of your individual style come through. Are you an oxford shirt kind of guy or an Italian sport shirt kind of guy? A sweater kind of guy or a vest kind of guy? There are many ways to appropriately and fashionably dress your torso. The following is a road map of shirt/sweater/vest categories (with a few of my favorites in parentheses):

- 3 button-down long-sleeved oxford shirts (try pink, blue-and-white-striped, and white).

- 3 Italian long-sleeved sport shirts (think basics in both fabric and pattern).

- 3 short-sleeved polo shirts (look for an interesting color that you like, maybe coral or celadon, in addition to white).

- 1 long-sleeved solid-color linen shirt.

- 1 cashmere long-sleeved polo (perhaps in gray or cream).

- 1 fine wool sweater with a small, discreet pattern.

- 2 cotton or cotton/linen sweaters (in solid colors—perhaps light yellow or navy).

- 2 vests (always very snappy! Think about a red cashmere sweater vest and a tan suede vest).

Shoes

Neither your wingtips nor your tennis shoes will cut it. Instead, try these three for shoe starters:

- 1 pair chocolate suede tie shoes.

- 1 pair oxblood leather loafers (no tassels!).

- 1 pair black leather sporty tie shoes (or the best—Gucci lug sole black leather buckle loafers).

Accessories

Accessorizing is an art and therefore can not be taught in any book. Here are a few thoughts as you perfect your own art form:

Belts

Your belt should match your shoes. Three good basics are a tan twisted leather, a brown alligator, and a black calfskin.

Socks

Be discreet in pattern. Be conservative in color. And make sure they are pulled high enough so that no leg shows.

Watch

Your best choice is a family heirloom or a new Breitling chronograph. Both are classic and individualistic. If neither is an option, sport a sport watch from a maker such as Swatch, Swiss Army, or Casio.

How to Tie a Bow Tie

"Formal dress lifts a man out of the ordinary, if he should be ordinary to begin with."

—*Roger Smith*

A PRETIED BOW tie is the evil twin brother of the clip-on tie. Is that you? Should that be anyone?!

A hand-tied bow tie is aesthetically more elegant. It flops softer and slightly askew, setting the mood for a close, dashing formal evening. To men, the man who ties his own is a can-do guy whom work colleagues can trust. To women, tying your own demonstrates the subtle flair that makes for a great lover.

But who on this planet can tie one of those thirty-inch strands of black silk, anyway? The fourth generation of eastern old money can. The fine private prep school–educated can. Those exposed to the A-list party circles can. And soon . . . you can.

Let's get a few excuses out of the way first. A hand-tied bow tie is no more expensive to purchase than a pretied bow tie (good-quality ones can be found for about $25). Hand-tied bow ties are readily available for purchase at a formal-wear store or fine men's clothing store near you. And, yes, you can and should own your own hand-tied bow tie even if you're renting the rest of your outfit. In fact, it is a great way to provide class to any rental tuxedo ensemble.

Follow the steps on pages 126 and 127 to master the art of tying a bow tie. Note: you may want to copy these pages and hang them on your mirror at eye level.

The diagrams are as you will see them in the mirror.

Before you start, adjust the length to your neck size with the contraption on the inside of the tie. The length of your bow tie determines how big or small it will be. Adjust to taste.

1. Begin with the left side two inches longer than the right.

2. Cross the left side over the right and then up and through the loop. Keep the knot loose at your throat.

3. This step makes the front bow. Fold the lower hanging end up and to the right to make the front of your bow tie. Make sure the folded side is to your right as shown.

4. Hold the folded bow and the knot with your left thumb and index finger. Cross the other end over the top of the folded bow. This will make a "hole" *behind* the folded bow and *ahead* of the knot. Place your right thumb and middle finger at the middle of the hanging end.

5. OK, this is the hard part. Fold the hanging ends together with your right-hand index finger and thumb. Leading with the fold, go behind the folded front bow and then left through the hole.

6. At this point you have a bundled mass of black silk sitting at your neck like a dead squirrel. Relax, your bow tie is fine; it just needs some work to finish it up. By pulling both folded ends, then both flat ends, you can tighten and smooth out the bow tie. Do this gently, or the tie will become undone.

It will take you several attempts to master the art of tying a bow tie. Until you have it down pat, allow thirty minutes to do it. You don't want to be running late and messing with a bow tie in front of a steamy bathroom mirror.

Laundry for Bachelors

"Out, damned spot! out, I say"

—*Lady Macbeth*

LIFE IS FILLED with cycles. Unfortunately, wash and dry cycles are among them, and there will be a time when there is no one else to handle them but you. Most red-blooded American males can pawn off their clothes cleaning on others for a majority of their natural life. The tricky time is post–high school, pre-marriage. That is when you are likely to get stuck separating the colors from the whites. And to make matters worse, that coincides with the time you must look your best.

Don't assume that dropping off clothes with your mom on the weekend is always an option. Don't assume that your girl-friend, or her less popular and ever-helpful roommate, will come to the rescue. Don't assume that cleaning ladies with laundry capability will always be a cost-conscious alternative. And don't assume that you can thrive without clean clothes as you did every spring break. Sure, all four of these are options—damn good options—that should be used, even abused.

But, life is indeed a cycle, and when it is your turn to stand before the white metal cleaning gods, chant this five-step mantra.

Step 1: Sort things out.

There is a high correlation between an organized, anal-retentive personality and successful laundry completion. If that is not you, pay careful attention to sorting things out. First, separate out any items whose tags say "dry clean only"—they mean it. Second, separate any other items that need special attention, such as a delicate wash cycle, a gentle detergent, or air-drying. Typical items needing special attention are sweaters

and any trousers other than khakis or blue jeans. Third, separate your remaining items into three piles: (1) bright and dark
colors such as blues, reds, and blacks, (2) pastels and near-
whites such as creams, striped oxford shirts, and white shirts
with printing, and (3) whites.

Take both the "dry clean only" and special attention stuff
to the dry cleaner. The remainder will make up about 80 percent of your laundry and is what we will deal with here.

Step 2: Perform a spot check.

A laundry rookie's biggest mistake is to go from sort to wash
without dealing with spots and stains. Simply, no special
prespotting results in no spot removal. Check all items for
stains, and treat any you find with a prewash stain remover
(such as *Shout* or *Spray 'n Wash*). Spray it liberally directly on
the stain or extra-dirty areas, and proceed.

Step 3: Wash away.

Wash the whites in one load using hot water. Wash the pastels
and near-whites in another load using warm water. Wash the
colors in a third load using cold water. If you have small loads,
it is OK to combine the whites and pastels/near-whites into a
single load and use warm water. When confused or in a hurry,
err on the side of using cold water.

Always use a general-purpose detergent (such as *Tide*). Get
in the habit of also adding a *color-safe* bleach (such as *Clorox 2*)
to all loads, which will brighten your clothes as well as help your
detergent clean tougher stains.

Step 4: Drip and dry.

Everybody's got some clothes that are just perfect, provided
they aren't put into the dryer. Take your beloved polo shirt or

jeans and hang them up to air-dry. Some items can be partially dried for five to ten minutes in the dryer and then air-dried for the remainder. When doing this, do not walk away from the dryer (and maybe even set a timer), as you will often forget, overdrying the treasured items. Throw everything else into the dryer and let 'em whirl. Toss a sheet of fabric softener (such as *Bounce* or *Snuggle*) in all dryer loads to reduce static cling as well as add a fresh, clean scent.

Step 5: Fold and iron.

Many items look OK (some even better) wrinkled, while others demand to be pressed. If you want to, or think you need to, press an item, see the following section. Folding is best done fresh out of the dryer before the clothes become unnecessarily wrinkled. Folding is also best done watching Letterman, a *Baywatch* rerun, or any good sports event.

How to Iron a Shirt

"It is only shallow people who do not
judge by appearances."

—*Oscar Wilde*

THE WRINKLED, casual look works with girls and on the weekends. It won't make as favorable an impression in everyday business life, where the demand for extra starch by most men in
power contributes to the continual erosion of the ozone layer.

As always, when time allows go with the pros—a good
laundry service in your neighborhood. Think of it this way:
since ironing a shirt will take you about twenty minutes, and
the cost to have one done at the dry cleaner is about $1, would
you work at the dry cleaner for $3 an hour?

But if you desire prisonlike manual labor, fire up some
ironing music (something with flair but not too distracting)
and crease along with me.

Step 1. Start with a clean shirt. Crisp garbage is still
garbage. If you've just washed the shirt, remove it from
the dryer (or hanger if air-drying) while it is still slightly
damp. If you fail to catch the shirt while it's still damp
(or if you broke the garbage rule and are recycling a
dirty shirt), dampen the shirt with a water sprayer or by
rolling it in a damp, clean towel. That steamer built into
the iron rarely works, so don't bother messing with it.

Step 2. Get out the iron and get it hot. Set the
temperature to the level indicated on the iron for your
shirt fabric at hand.

Step 3. Set up the ironing board. If you're right-handed,
the narrow end is to your left, and vice versa. (Incidentally,

like borrowing the proverbial cup of sugar, borrowing an ironing board from appealing neighbors is a great way to grab an introduction. They see you as a cute-guy-trying-to-make-it-on-his-own-for-a-while type.) If all else fails, put a clean bath towel on top of your kitchen counter.

Step 4. Lay the shirt face down, with the arms hanging to the sides. Iron the back of the shirt. Since mess-ups here will show the least (provided you keep your jacket on), use this opportunity to get comfortable with your stroke. (Notwithstanding the ozone layer, a little spray starch makes the work go smoothly.) Turn the shirt over and iron the front two sides.

Step 5. Lay out each sleeve flat, making a crease from the shoulder to the cuff. Iron each side holding the same line you have established. The cuffs are critical, as they show even if you keep your jacket on. The cuffs also burn easily, so use repetitive long strokes rather than holding the iron in a single spot for long.

Step 6. Iron the front placket—the part with the buttons—ironing around the buttons (that's what the nose of the iron is for) rather than over them (or you will be using the following "How to Sew On a Button" section more than you would like).

Step 7. We're rounding third and heading for home now. Last is the collar. Flip up the collar and begin by ironing the underneath. Then flip the collar over and iron the outside of the collar, again exercising special care not to linger too long and cause a burn.

Step 8. Let the shirt cool down for a few minutes. Slip it on and go forth and prosper in unwrinkled excellence.

How to Sew On a Button

"Button, button, who's got the button?"

—*Nursery rhyme*

THERE IS NOTHING more boring than learning how to sew on a button. Of all the survival skills you need to know, this is by far the least sexy. The best advice, then, is the simplest: get somebody else to do it for you. Possibilities include your girlfriend, the local dry cleaner, the hotel tailor, your mom, the neighbor down the hall . . . anyone with needle and thread.

If it has to be you, here is how you do it.

As with all tasks, begin by gathering your instruments and materials. Keep a standard-size needle around (about 1½ inches long), a sampling of threads (black, navy, white, and khaki can get all jobs done), and some spare buttons (you will need a broad sampling, including the little white buttons that work on dress shirts, other small shirt buttons in the colors that would match most of your casual shirts, some medium-size black buttons that can work on the waist of pants, and a few larger buttons for suits and other jackets). Try not to lose the original buttons, as they may be difficult to match. If they look loose, cut them off and pin them to the inside of the garment or put them in your dresser or desk. It is a good idea to have a storage tin with these supplies where you can also toss the spare buttons that accompany many clothing purchases.

Step 1. Thread the needle with about thirty-six inches of thread. Double the thread over and knot it at the end.

Step 2. Locate the holes from where the button used to be. From the inside of the garment push the needle halfway through the front of the garment. Place the button on the needle and push the needle the rest of the way through the fabric. Pull the needle until the knot stops it, pulling gently toward the end.

Step 3. Select a different hole in the button—preferably the one diagonal to the first hole—and push the needle and thread back through to the other side of the garment. Do not pull the thread too tight.

Step 4. Repeat Step 3 until you have about six inches of thread remaining. Make sure to end with the needle on a downstroke (i.e., back under the button). Wrap the remaining thread a couple of times tightly around the back of the button.

Step 5. Tie a knot, and cut the excess thread. Put the needle away for another fun, button-sewing day.

Part VII

Spare Skills

Conversation Made Easy

"Talk low, talk slow, and don't say too much."
—*John Wayne*

THERE ARE TWO ways to be the life of the party: (1) be witty, gregarious, courteous, well-read, and informed about a wide variety of current events and high and popular culture, or (2) fake it. Given that you are reading this section, the first option is likely not an option. So, let's talk about faking it. As you engage in chitchat, keep in mind these fundamental truths.

Everybody thinks he or she is fascinating.

Ask people to tell you about themselves—their background, their work, their family, their hobbies, their date. Listen with curiosity to their stories and ideas. At the very least, practice the skill of *looking* as if you are listening while you mentally undress the most attractive women at the party. Your jabbermate will never remember that he did all the talking. Instead, he'll recall fondly how interested (and therefore *interesting*) you were.

Flattery will get you everywhere.

Even the most cynical among us are ready to believe the best about ourselves. Flattery will get you everywhere (it's worked on you, believe me). To be effective, the well-placed compliment should be attuned to the particular recipient and conversation. Compliment the host on his or her home and food, the gorgeous woman on her outfit, the accomplished professional on his or her job, the opinionated conversationalist on his or her thoughts. If you choose the right compliments—that is, ones the recipient already believes but is eager to hear affirmed—you generally can not overdo it.

Agreement beats disagreement.

People respond to people in whom they can see themselves. When you are trying to make a good initial impression, try to avoid a spirited debate. Federally funded programs—off-limits. Women in the workplace—leave it alone. Gays in the military—too hot to touch. Instead, look for topics of shared interest and opinion. Even the most disparate of personalities can find sports and movies that they each saw and similarly loved or hated.

It's surprising how little you need to know.

A little knowledge goes a long way. Perusing a few well-chosen books can take the place of real substantive knowledge (at least for purposes of cocktail chat).

If you snoozed your way through years of art, literature, architecture, and music appreciation classes, pick up Daniel Boorstin's *The Creators* to refresh your memory of all in just one book. If your recollection of history is sketchy, check out any volume of *The Story of Civilization* by Will and Ariel Durant. A great book on law is *The Brethren* by Bob Woodward and Scott Armstrong. If the world of science is an impenetrable mystery to you, try Stephen Jay Gould's *Ever Since Darwin* or Stephen Hawking Jr.'s *A Brief History of Time*. And the basics of the current technology landscape are nicely set forth in *Being Digital* by Nicolas Negroponte and *The Road Ahead* by Bill Gates.

By reading just one of these books each month, within six months you can build yourself a solid foundation of all the art, literature, architecture, music, history, law, science, and technology that you missed when you were in your "Why would I ever care about this stuff, anyway?" years.

To keep up to date from now on, do as I do:

The Culture Cheat Sheet

1. Business, national, and international events—Read the front two summary columns of the *Wall Street Journal.*

2. Sports—If you need help here, you are a lost cause.

3. TV, movies, and theater—Read *Entertainment Weekly.*

4. Literature—Read the Sunday Book Review in the *New York Times* (who has time to actually *read* the books?!) every so often.

5. Popular culture—Read *Vanity Fair* and *Details* monthly.

6. Music—Read *Rolling Stone* monthly.

7. On-line world—Check out *America Online* weekly.

Diversity of sources impresses. Name-dropping the source of a tidbit into the conversation lends credibility to your opinions and interest to your experiences.

It is always easier, and often more fun, to *appear* impressive, than to be impressive.

How to Clean Your Bathroom for Guests in Five Minutes

> "What separates two people most profoundly is a different sense and degree of cleanliness."
>
> —*Friedrich Wilhelm Nietzsche*

OK, so you don't care if your bathroom is clean. In fact, you think it *is* clean. But people do notice. Just as Nietzsche says, there are two types of people: the clean and the unclean. This is not the fraternity anymore.

Who are the usual suspects who will judge you by the cleanliness of your bathroom? Your in-laws just called and are stopping by. Your date surprisingly agrees to stay over for the first time. You are having a few work colleagues over to watch the sports finals and eat pizza. All these people thought you were a classy guy before your show of hospitality. What could go wrong? That's right—your bathroom.

Five minutes, I promise. Put on the full versions of "American Pie" by Don McClean, "Paradise by the Dashboard Light" by Meat Loaf, or "Roundabout" by Yes, and the job will be done *halfway* into the song. It just might become your favorite pre-entertainment ritual.

Your Tools

1. All-purpose spray cleaner
2. Glass cleaner
3. Paper towels
4. Air freshener

Your Plan of Action

1. Throw all dirty towels into the clothes basket (or, if you must, onto the floor of your closet). Put out a fresh hand towel.

2. If you have a bath rug, shake it out the window (or if you must, in the shower or tub basin). Wipe up all loose hairs and visible dirt from the floor with the all-purpose cleaner and the paper towels.

3. Hide all toiletries and miscellaneous junk that you have around the sink behind the closed shower curtain.

4. Spray the entire toilet—under lids, inside the bowl—with the all-purpose cleaner. Wipe up with paper towels, making sure to rub hard to remove any discolored areas. Flush the toilet a couple of times to clear the suds.

5. Spray the sink and sink counter, including the soap dish, with the all-purpose cleaner. Apply elbow grease. This area is critical.

6. Clean the mirror with glass cleaner.

7. Put out a fresh bar of hand soap or make sure the liquid soap dispenser is near-full. (If the bar of soap is natural and decorative, such as a beeswax bar, award yourself bonus points.)

8. Empty the wastebasket.

9. Lightly spray air freshener.

10. *Do not use the bathroom before the guests arrive.*

Warning: This five-minute bathroom cleanup is for show only. It is not meant as a substitute for real sanitary cleaning. Of course, real cleaning is best done by someone other than you. A cleaning person is recommended on a once-every-two-to-four-weeks basis.

Remove That Stain!

"No use crying over spilled milk."

—Proverb

MODERN MEN MAKE mishaps. A life unspilled upon is a life not worth living.

So, keep on eating pizza over your lap while you're lying on the couch. Keep swirling red wine over your rug in front of the fireplace. Keep balancing your cigar on your pine chest of drawers. Just know how to handle the terrible ten stains listed here.

In all cases, act fast. There is a greater than fifty-fifty chance of successfully removing all stains if they are caught fresh. Your first step is to soak up any excess liquid. Use a clean, white cloth to prevent any discoloring. Blotting is the spot-removal motion you are seeking. Nobody really knows how to do it, but it isn't rubbing or scrubbing—these motions will spread and grind in the stain, making it worse, not better. Start blotting with cold water, then continue as noted in the table.

The more expensive or irreplaceable the soiled item, the more you need expert help. With clothes, blankets, or other fabrics, get to a fine dry cleaner as soon as possible. With carpets, reach out and contact carpet cleaning specialists listed in your local yellow pages.

If you remember only one thing, remember to keep an all-purpose stain remover around your place. When mishaps happen, grab the stain-remover bottle and read the back panel.

If the stains don't come out—know when to forget about it and take your loss like a man.

The Stain	The Action
Alcohol	Vinegar and water
Blood	Cold water and soap
Chocolate	Nonbleach detergent
Cigar burn	Accept it as character
Coffee	Vinegar and water mix
Grease	Baking soda or club soda
Ink	Nonbleach detergent
Lipstick	A modern notch on the belt—keep it
Red wine	Club soda
Urine	Ammonia and water mix

How to Paint a Room

"Painting is very easy when you don't know
how, but very difficult when you do."

—*Edgar Degas*

WHITE WALLS AND minimalist black lacquer furniture? Hey, '80s Man, that is long out, along with slick-backed hair, label fixation, bond trading, and sushi as one of the four food groups. It also screams boring, lowly apartment dweller. The millennium is about expression and painting a room is the easiest and cheapest way to change an entire apartment. Do anything from bold, striking colors to classical, formal schemes—but do something. Without expensive furniture or art, a fresh infusion of color can make the plainest space into an inviting and impressive home. Colors express who you are and can impact how you feel.

Step 1: Preparing the Room

Begin by protecting everything that could be splattered by the paint. Do this by moving items out of the room to be painted or to the center of the room and covering them with sheets of plastic. Remove all picture hangers from the walls, hardware from windows and doors, and light switch and electric outlet plates. Cover heating and air-conditioning ducts. Tape down sheets of plastic or heavy paper on the floors to protect the surface.

The walls must be clean and smooth. To get the walls ready you may need to (1) remove stains (use an all-purpose cleaner and apply a stain-killing sealer if any stain residue remains), (2) patch peeling paint (scrape away loose paint with a putty knife, apply Spackle, and sand till the surface is smooth when dry), (3) fill nail holes (fill the holes just past even with Spackle), or (4) patch holes or indentations (scrape away loose wallboard, cover with a repair patch if cracking exists, cover the hole or repair patch with filling compound, and sand until the repair is even with the wall when dry).

The last step in preparing the room is applying primers and sealers. A primer is used to cover areas that have been repaired or when a lighter color paint is being applied over a darker wall. Only a single primer coat is necessary. A sealer is used over wood surfaces such as baseboards, doors, or cabinets. A sealer helps close the breathability of the wood so the paint takes to the surface evenly.

Step 2: Painting the Ceiling and Walls

Begin by painting the ceiling of your room in the farthest corner from the entry door. Use a two-inch trim brush to paint far enough into the center of the ceiling to begin using a standard three-quarter-inch nap roller. Paint the ceiling in three-foot-by-three-foot sections using the roller. When applying paint with a roller, begin with diagonal strokes, followed by up-and-down strokes, and finish with horizontal strokes.

Once you have completed the ceiling, move to the walls. Again, begin in the corner farthest away from the door and proceed in the same manner as with the ceiling. With the walls, always start at the top of your section, stroking downward to avoid dripping paint. Before the edges of a section are dry, cut in with the roller and begin the next section.

Step 3: Painting the Trim

Trim may be air duct gratings, baseboards, moldings, window edges, or doors. If the trim will be painted a different color from the walls, apply masking or other prestuck brown tape to separate the trim.

Paint Design Tips

- Neutral walls, whether a shade of white or lighter color, reflect light, making a room appear larger and ceilings higher. Best for a living room, bedroom, or kitchen.

- Colored walls, whether deep or bright, catch the eye, making a room seem more intimate and more alive. They are excellent in a dining room, study, or bathroom.

- There are four levels of paint shine: flat, eggshell, gloss, and high gloss. Gloss paints are most washable, so they are good for the kitchen, the bathroom, and trim. Eggshell is the best all-purpose choice. Flat is often best when using deep or bright colors.

- There are no fewer than 100 shades of off-white and cream. Try to take it seriously, but don't obsess for more than ten minutes before making your selection.

- Look at the dark end of the paint sample strip which indicates the base colors used to make up the shades on the strip. This may make it easier to choose among your finalists.

- Paint samples can be deceiving. Pros select a few shades and purchase sample quarts of the paint to test. Paint cardboard sheets and tape them to the to-be-painted-room walls. Colors look much different on a twelve-foot wall from the way they do on a one-inch square. And colors look different in daylight from the way they do in evening artificial light.

- Dare to use color. You will most likely love your bold step. If you don't like it after a few weeks—change it. It's only a few bucks and a little more time.

- Air ducts can be most easily painted with spray paint.

- Baseboards are best painted using a two-inch trim brush.

- Moldings, if intricate, will require a stenciling brush (a brush that looks like an old-time shaving cream applicator). Use circular motions to penetrate the areas.

- Windows are difficult. Use a tapered one-inch brush. Open and close the windows every hour or so during painting to stop them from sticking. Leave windows open a bit for seven days after painting. Clean paint off the glass when it's dry using a putty knife followed by glass cleaner and paper towels.

- Doors should be removed from their hinges and placed flat on sawhorses to be painted.

Dealing with Stress

"Archie don't know how to worry
without getting upset."

—*Edith Bunker,* All in the
Family

DON'T THINK YOU'RE stressed? Denial, my friend, is one of the telltale signs. For our purposes, assume you are under stress. And although it can be the fuel of your success, too much high octane has made even space shuttles blow.

Question: Which are often caused by stress?

A. Headaches

B. Acne

C. Impotence

D. Fatigue

Answer: E, All of the above. And more.

Muscle aches, insomnia, nausea . . . if cancer is the silent killer, then stress is the visible annoyer. So, how do you harness your stress and make it your friend?

First, identify the source of your stress. To solve any problem, you must first identify it. Be introspective and honest with yourself when determining the cause of your stress. Is it money? Women? Work? Family? Is stress itself stressing you out? If you're like most men, each will be your number-one source of stress at *some* point in your life.

Stress over money is generally due to lack of it. It's a stress that will strike you time and again. Woman stress generally revolves around not having one, or having the wrong one. Work stress will rear its ugly head in many ways—bad boss, big project due, problems with a coworker, pushing for a promotion.

Family stress is never-ending, as your family's individual stresses become your stress. And finally, stress breeds more stress, which is all the more reason to catch it early and deal with it effectively.

Second, put a plan in place to relieve the stress. The goal of any plan is to feel better in the short term while you arrive at a long-term solution.

One trick to feeling better in the short term is to ask yourself: "What is the worst thing that could happen?" Most times the answer is not that awful. And most times the real probability of the worst's happening is small. Another trick is to focus on the positives in your life. Working ninety hours a week for months on end? You probably have few financial worries. Career not going great? Focus on your beautiful babe. Try to put the stress in perspective. Simply, your short-term objective is to relax. Do what works for you.

Long-term solutions are as varied as the individual. A few things tend to help many people, such as a regular exercise routine, a daily thirty-minute meditation or an extra hour of sleep, or reserving every other Saturday to do whatever you want. But the root of your stress may be even more serious—you're in a dead-end job or a relationship that shouldn't or can't be saved. The only way to relieve this stress is to deal with the cause. There isn't any shortcut.

For help identifying the problem, talk to your best friend, girlfriend (unless she is the problem!), or parents. If you don't feel that any of your best confidants is up to the task, seek professional help. Often a counselor can help you see things very clearly in just a few one-hour sessions. And don't feel stigmatized—more people have talked things through with a counselor than you think (heck, in some circles it's *de rigueur*).

The solution to the problem is both easy and hard. Easy to arrive at, hard to follow through on. If you have really identified the problem, the solution will follow. Not sure you want to marry your girlfriend? Answer seems clear. Not happy in your job? Answer seems clear. Relationship with your parents no longer close? Answer seems clear. The hard part to a long-term solution is having the guts to carry it out.

Healthy Traveling

"Travel is glamorous only in retrospect."
—*Paul Theroux*

YES, BECOMING A 100,000-mile traveler has its advantages—but, no, living healthy and looking good are not among them. Only sound, disciplined habits can overcome the fatty foods, lack of sleep, cramped, dry flight quarters, and irregular schedule that besiege the frequent traveler. But just as Mel Gibson looked good as the *Road Warrior,* so can you by following these travel tips.

The Flight

Health Trip

You missed lunch rushing to get out the door, and your stomach won't wait for a real meal. Long check-in lines, flight delays, no pay phones, crying babies, and your position in a coach middle seat left you frazzled, desperately in need of a drink to take the edge off. Just a few minutes afterward, those two tiny bags of peanuts and two alcoholic beverages have stuck you with ⅓ your daily calories. Worse yet, you are still hungry and also a little tipsy.

Health Tip

Pass on the premeal snacks, as well as on the meal desserts. Carry fat-free granola bars in your briefcase for hunger emergencies. Select the lighter-fare meal when possible, fruit plate for breakfast and the chicken or fish option for dinner. Do not double-dip on meals: if you have a business dinner, skip the in-flight offering. And no in-flight alcohol, period. Have the drink when you'll enjoy it more.

Five High-Skies Healthy Habits

1. Pressurized cabins and caffeine from coffee and soda cause dehydration—drink at least one glass of water per one hour of flight time.

2. Cramped seating hurts circulation and back muscles—walk the aisle a few times each hour or so of the flight.

3. Long stretches of sleep on planes will leave you groggy—try a twenty-minute nap for maximum alertness and restfulness.

4. Skin and eyes dry out—splash water on your face, put lotion on your hands, and put saline drops in your eyes before, during, and after your flight.

5. Joints and feet swell—if you have any arthritic conditions you might want to take an anti-inflammatory (such as Aleve) prior to your flight.

The Hotel

Health Trip

You arrive exhausted, mentally and physically, and have the craving to treat yourself. The road is hard, but at least while on it, you rationalize, you should treat yourself like a king. You order the shrimp cocktail, New York strip medium rare, whipped garlic potatoes, and chocolate-chip cheesecake. You plop down on the big, comfy bed and select the recent action blockbuster on pay-per-view. Stop.

Health Tip

Try to keep some manly discipline. How about the lighter fare, or better yet, focusing on having a big, healthy breakfast the next morning? The movie? Usually you will fall asleep, miss the end, and be tired in your morning meeting. Skip it all. Call the babe to say hello, answer your E-mail, enjoy a good novel, or catch up on some sleep. If you really have it in you, hit the health club or work out in your room (see page 91 for my recommended twenty-minute no-equipment workout).

Manly Possessions

> "Whoever dies with the most toys wins."
>
> —*T-shirt slogan*

IT'S BEEN SAID that a man is the sum total of his possessions. It's also been said that you are what you own. Shallow exaggeration? Perhaps. But you get the point—you need a lot of stuff. Not just any stuff, though. The right stuff. You need the stuff that screams, "I'm THE MAN!" and you need to stay away from the stuff that screams, "I'm a WANNA-BE!"

The great thing about most possessions is that they can be *purchased*, transforming your image before the Visa bill even arrives. They are consumer durables, and they serve to make your life more comfortable while they impress others.

Certain tangible possessions universally rule—a Gulfstream V., a Bentley Turbo, an Aspen ski house. But it will do you a lot more good to focus on goodies you can actually attain. These are the items that can be acquired by the average guy with above-average luck and commitment to getting them.

Be a more-is-more kind of a guy. See how many of these thirty indispensable items you can acquire by the time you are thirty. (Approximate costs are noted in parentheses.)

1. A Breitling chronograph watch with leather strap ($3,000)

2. A very long black cashmere designer overcoat ($2,000—and be sure to get the *walk* down)

3. A really good haircut ($75)

4. A natural brown leather reading club chair and ottoman ($3,000)

5. A worn, wool player's baseball cap from your favorite team ($15)

6. A Tiffany's monogrammed sterling silver belt buckle ($250)

7. An antique cigar cutter (up to $1,000)

8. A Mitsubishi Picture-in-Picture thirty-five-inch-screen television ($1,500)

9. The latest palm-top PC ($1,000)

10. The smallest cell phone ($200)

11. A video camera ($750—there *are* things to record before your wedding or first child)

12. A cherry-wood sleigh bed (up to $5,000)

13. A Pelikan roller ball pen ($175)

14. A Porsche 911 ($80,000)

15. A navy blue power Armani suit ($1,750)

16. A big, bad, loud stereo (spend as much as you can afford—your stereo is the most important sign of machismo other than your car)

17. A manly CD collection (priceless, and you'll know it when you hear it)

18. A multimedia top-of-the-line home PC ($3,000)

19. Cool blazer buttons (up to $500—go for antique, monogrammed, or those from your alma mater)

20. Good sunglasses that are really *you* ($250)

21. Golf clubs—Ping irons and Callaway graphites ($1,500 a set)

22. Your own apartment (up to $2,000 a month)

23. A custom-made Sulka sea island cotton French-cuff shirt ($400) and coordinating Hermes tie ($140)

24. A stock portfolio of growth companies (the sky's the limit)

25. A sterling silver–framed five-by-seven-inch photo of you as a baby ($150 for the frame)

Certain possessions cannot be purchased. They are, however, well worth acquiring. They include:

26. A firm handshake

27. The ability to look others in the eye

28. Dignity

29. A moral code

30. Self-confidence

Freedom

"Man is free at the moment he wishes to be."
—*Voltaire*

THE ULTIMATE GOAL when it comes to survival skills is freedom from having to do most of the stuff in this book. Only when the modern man no longer has to worry about his survival can he truly thrive.

Freedom comes on a silver platter when you retain a full staff—your chauffeur, maid, cook, personal trainer, and garçon should be able to spring you from life's little details. Freedom comes for the regular guy, though, from good old-fashioned growing up. A mature man naturally cares less about impressing others, getting ahead, and living the good life, and more about meaningful work, deep friendships, true love, interesting hobbies, and giving something back.

Freedom is not, as the song says, just another word for nothing left to lose. Freedom is the ultimate step to making your mark in style.

About the Author

DONN M. DAVIS is a media company executive and venture capitalist. He has also served as chief legal counsel for the Chicago Cubs baseball team. He lives with his wife and baby son in downtown Chicago.